Royal Botanic Gardens Kew

THE KEW GARDENER'S GUIDE TO

GROWING ORCHIDS

Royal Botanic Gardens Kew

THE KEW GARDENER'S GUIDE TO

GROWING ORCHIDS

THE ART AND SCIENCE TO GROW YOUR OWN ORCHIDS

PHILIP SEATON

FRANCES LINCOLN

Contents

Introduction to growing orchids

THE VALUE OF ORCHIDS

Why this obsession with orchids? Clearly one of the attractions is the spectacular diversity of their flowers, ranging from large and showy cattleyas and cool elegant sprays of moth orchids (*Phalaenopsis*) to tiny, jewel-like *Lepanthes*. With more than 26,000 species identified to date (and probably many more to come), orchids can be found growing on all continents apart from Antarctica. The Orchidaceae (the orchid family) makes up around 9 per cent of the world's plant biodiversity, with the majority of species living in the tropics. Some have evolved to grow high in the forest canopy, where they are subject to the full power of the sun's rays, while others grow on the humid and shady forest floor. Yet more inhabit the more temperate climes of English meadows and South African fynbos.

Orchids are beautiful, magical, exotic and exude charisma. Often, however, they are thought to be difficult to grow. There are, of course, species that can be challenging, attract the specialist grower and are considered to be strictly greenhouse subjects. Over recent years, however, it has become increasingly apparent that a wide range of orchids can be successfully grown in the home. Indeed, they are often much tougher than the average house plant.

A little history

On 17 February 1899, the auctioneers Protheroe & Morris of London offered 100,000 plants of Princess Alexandra's oncidium (*Oncidium alexandrae*) for sale. Today, the scale of orchid imports in the nineteenth century are difficult to comprehend. Literally millions of orchids must have been removed from the wild, vast numbers dying in transit even before they reached European shores. Nurserymen such as Frederick Sanders in the UK housed their imports in vast ranges of greenhouses, sending collectors around the world in search of ever more novel specimens. Many of those intrepid orchid hunters died in pursuit of their goals: some of tropical diseases such as malaria and yellow fever; others suffered accidental deaths; and some were murdered.

OPPOSITE Orchids can be grown with a wide range of other plants to produce an attractive effect. Here at the Kew Orchid Festival, moth orchids can be seen peeking through the foliage of *Hoya linearis* and various ferns, bromeliads and begonias.

Miltonia moreliana, with its dark plum sepals and petals, is particularly desirable; once considered a variety of *M. spectabilis*, it is now a species in its own right.

Cambria orchids are increasingly available in almost every colour of the rainbow, including a vibrant orange. There is something for everyone.

This was a time of 'orchid mania', when orchids were largely the preserve of the rich, who sometimes paid vast sums of money for particularly desirable specimens, and assembled large private collections containing thousands of plants. Initially, growers did not understand how to cultivate these treasures. Out of those that did survive their long sea voyages, large numbers perished in hot and steamy stove houses, even though many came from cool and misty cloud forests. As information became more widely available, orchids began to be cultivated in conditions better reflecting their natural habitats.

Today, those enormous collections of orchids looked after by teams of gardeners for wealthy patrons are a distant memory. With a few notable exceptions such as botanical gardens, few large private collections remain. Instead, today orchids are within the reach of everyone.

Moth orchids (*Phalaenopsis*), once thought to be an orchid strictly for the warm greenhouse, are probably the world's most popular pot plant. Millions are grown in commercial nurseries for sale in retail outlets. Once you have cut your orchid-growing teeth, on a moth orchid perhaps, there is a wide range of interesting species and hybrids available to tempt the discerning enthusiast, and something to suit everyone's pocket.

The pages that follow include many of the commonly grown species and hybrids, together with a generous sprinkling of some of the more rarely encountered specimens that you may

A word about names

Aside from being unfamiliar, as our understanding of the relations between plants moves forward it is inevitable that, much to the chagrin of growers, the names of orchid species sometimes change: *Odontoglossum* suddenly becomes *Oncidium*, *Sophronitis* becomes *Cattleya*. To avoid confusion, the most up-to-date terms have been used throughout this book and, where appropriate, the older names included in brackets.

Despite its scientific name of *Disa uniflora*, pride of Table Mountain often has two or more spectacular, almost fluorescent, blooms.

wish to search out. They are, however, just a sample of the enormous diversity of plants that make up the orchid family. Be warned – orchids are addictive, and once hooked it is likely that, in common with growers of old, you will want to find and grow ever more examples of these botanical treasures.

MAN-MADE ORCHIDS

Hybridizers are continually striving to improve on nature. To date, more than 70,000 crosses have been registered with the Royal Horticultural Society (RHS), the international body responsible for naming orchid hybrids. Bigger flowers, more flowers, rounder flowers, different colours, spots and stripes . . . fashions come and go. The public is always looking for something new and exciting. Windowsill orchids should be tolerant of a wide range of temperatures, be vigorous and easy to grow.

Orchids are notoriously promiscuous. Because they often rely on specific pollinators, they tend to have few barriers in nature to cross-pollination. Not only is it frequently possible to make crosses between different species in the same genus, but it is also often feasible to create crosses between species in different, related genera. This can make the naming of such intergeneric crosses difficult. It is simple enough when crossing a *Laelia* with a *Cattleya*: the resulting hybrid is a × *Laeliocattleya*. However, things become much more complicated when three or four (and occasionally more) genera are involved. Unsurprisingly, a host of new names has been invented for the different hybrid genera.

Commercial growers have overcome this problem in one group of related genera by calling them all cambrias. Originally applied to × *Vuylstekeara* (now × *Oncidopsis*) Cambria, a famous intergeneric hybrid registered in 1931, the term cambria is now applied to a wide range of intergeneric hybrids sold around the world as compact windowsill plants that have similar cultural requirements (see Cambria, page 54). The most desirable varieties have been selected and propagated in large numbers by tissue culture.

At one time a florist's favourite, individual boxed cymbidium flowers were sold for special occasions, including Valentine's Day, and a single spike of flowers could last for up to six weeks. The problem was that with large, rounded pseudobulbs and long, strap-like leaves, standard cymbidiums were often very large plants indeed, and could be difficult to accommodate. Hybridizers have since produced a range of charming miniatures, including some with pendulous flower spikes, that are suitable for the home.

Today, moth orchids (*Phalaenopsis*) seem to appear in the background of almost every television play and studio interview, lending an air of sophistication. Until comparatively recently, they were available only in white or deep rose-pink. Today, they are seen for sale in a fabulous array of colour schemes . . . and sometimes flowers that have been artificially coloured with a lurid blue dye. There is something for everyone, and a whole new range of charming miniatures is becoming more widely available. Nurseries are able to manipulate their growing conditions so that moth orchids can be induced to flower at any time of the year.

In contrast to the cool elegance of moth orchids, the big blowsy blooms of cattleyas have often been disparaged as being 'chocolate-box orchids', and even a little vulgar. For many of us however, their flamboyant blooms are quite simply gorgeous. Although, because of their size, many are normally considered to be plants for the greenhouse or conservatory, by making crosses with some of the smaller species in the genus, hybridizers have produced a kaleidoscope of brilliantly coloured, miniature gems suitable for growing on a windowsill. These tough, compact plants have foliage that is usually less than 15cm/6in long, and they will flower two or three times a year.

Finally, love them or hate them, tropical slipper orchids (*Paphiopedilum* and *Phragmipedium*) certainly have personality. Often resembling carnivorous plants, typically they lure potential pollinators into falling into the pouch-like lip, only allowing them to escape imprisonment by squeezing through a narrow gap while being smeared with greasy pollen. Hybridizers have now bred a range of plants with larger, splendid, long-lasting flowers, in shades of yellow and brown, which shine as if they have been polished.

WHERE DO ORCHIDS GROW?

Orchids have a diverse range of life cycles, reflecting their differing habitats. Time researching your plants is time well spent when deciding how best to grow them.

Sobralias (left) exhibit a sympodial mode of growth, the rhizome producing a series of new canes each year. Vandas (right) are typical monopodial plants, which gradually increase in size as new fans of leaves are added to each growing tip.

Orchid growth patterns

Orchids display two distinct growth patterns. The majority are described as being sympodial, that is to say that a sometimes-branched rhizome produces a succession of shoots that stop growing when they mature. One or more new shoots will then appear from the base of the old growth. To conserve water, many sympodial orchids have swollen stems, called pseudobulbs, which can tide them over during periods of reduced water availability.

Monopodial orchids comprise a fan of leaves, which is a single shoot that grows indefinitely from its apex. Occasionally, side shoots appear and the plant develops into a clump. Roots grow directly from the stem. Monopodial orchids do not produce pseudobulbs. There are always exceptions to such simple classifications, and the tuberous orchids are not obviously monopodial or sympodial.

Epiphytic orchids

The majority of tropical species, indeed the majority of orchids, are epiphytes, that is to say that they grow on the branches and trunks of trees. Others grow on rocks, in which case they are referred to as lithophytes. In Latin America epiphytes are sometimes referred to as *parasitos*, but in truth they are not parasitic on their arboreal hosts, merely using the trees to help access the sunshine. Although many orchids are said to be plants of the 'tropical rainforest', there are, in fact, many different types of rainforest, each with its own distinctive assemblage of epiphytes, including lichens, mosses, ferns and, in the Americas, bromeliads. Cloud forests have vegetation that is constantly dripping with water, and the sheer weight of epiphytes (not just the orchids) can cause a branch to break and crash to the ground. Cloud forests host orchids with different cultural requirements to those growing in a tropical dry forest, for example.

Flowers and their pollination
Charles Darwin was captivated by the amazing diversity of pollination strategies found in the Orchidaceae. Typically pollinated by insects, many tropical species are visited by beautiful iridescent euglossine bees. Others are pollinated by hummingbirds, moths or butterflies. Some blooms emit delicious perfumes, while others attract carrion flies by smelling of rotting meat.

Orchid flowers all conform to the same basic plan: three sepals, three petals and a central column. The ovary containing the ovules (eggs) is located behind the sepals and petals. The flowers are usually 'resupinate', that is, during development they rotate through 180 degrees so that the third petal – the lip (or labellum) – points downwards. Often the lip is large and showy, and it acts as a flag to attract and guide pollinators. In the case of slipper orchids (*Cypripedium*, *Paphiopedilum* and *Phragmipedium*), the lip is modified to form a pouch. But diversity rules, and in masdevallias and disas the pollinator is attracted by the large, brightly coloured sepals, and the lip is reduced to a tiny 'tongue'.

At first sight, orchid flowers can present the grower with a puzzle. Where is the pollen? Unlike the flowers of more familiar plants such as buttercups (*Ranunculus*) or tulips (*Tulipa*), yellow powdery pollen is not located on the tips of the stamens; instead, it is either found aggregated into clumps called pollinia, hidden behind an anther cap at the tip of the column, or in slipper orchids it is found as two greasy lumps either side of the column. A sticky pool of stigmatic fluid is located on the underside of the column, behind and separated from the pollinia by a small flap (the rostellum). In contrast, the stigma of a slipper orchid is a shiny disc on the underside of the column, hidden inside the pouch (see also Pollinating orchids, page 124).

FROM TOP TO BOTTOM *Cymbidium* hybrid, *Phalaenopsis bellina*, *Masdevallia* Cassiope, *Laelia anceps*

Leaves can give a clue as to the growing conditions that a plant requires. The thick leathery leaves of many *Cattleya* species are an adaptation to living high in the canopy, where they may be subject to the full force of the midday sun. In this sense, they have much in common with cacti, with similar physiological adaptations. Fleshy cylindrical leaves found in other species are designed to further reduce water loss. Large thin leaves are usually associated with shade-loving plants.

The roots of epiphytic species can be a source of some confusion as they lack root hairs. Instead, when dry, they have a white or a silvery appearance because of a special outer layer of cells called the velamen, which acts like a sponge and becomes green when wet due to the core of the root containing the photosynthetic pigment chlorophyll. When actively growing, these roots have green or reddish tips.

Terrestrial orchids

As the name implies, terrestrial orchids grow on the ground and in the soil. Usually found in the shady understorey, the roots of tropical terrestrial orchids are generally relatively conventional, with obviously hairy roots, at least in part. In the case of tropical slipper orchids (*Paphiopedilum*), however, they are severely reduced in number when compared with the fibrous root systems found in other herbaceous plants, and special care is needed as these roots are not easily replaced if allowed to rot and die.

Terrestrial orchids from temperate zones differ from their tropical counterparts in that they have to survive either a cold northern winter or a hot, dry, Mediterranean-type summer. After building up a starchy food reserve in a tuber or a rhizome, plants lose their leaves before entering a period of dormancy. Plants that lose their leaves in autumn are described as being summergreen. Those that lose their leaves in advance of a hot dry summer are wintergreen.

GROWING ORCHIDS IN THE HOME

One of the great advantages of growing orchids in the house is that they can easily receive individual care on a daily basis. Generally speaking, if you have the space, an orchid can be grown somewhere in your home, although you will probably have to clean its leaves from time to time (see Cleaning, pages 31–2). Not only will this remove unsightly dirt, but it will also increase the amount of light that the leaves receive (and possibly remove pests).

Indoor culture of orchids is becoming more and more popular, especially in view of increasing energy prices, which mean that heating a greenhouse can be expensive. After starting out with a moth orchid (*Phalaenopsis*) on the windowsill, indoor growers often graduate to more demanding subjects. A surprising array of rare and beautiful orchid species that have been grown in the home are often seen at orchid shows.

Temperature

As a general guideline, cool growing orchids require a winter minimum temperature of 10–13°C/50–55°F, with a summer maximum of 24°C/75°F. Those plants that require a little more heat can be grown under intermediate conditions with a minimum temperature of 13–15°C/55–59°F and a summer maximum of 24°C/75°F. Plants originating in warmer climes should be grown in an environment with a minimum temperature of 18°C/65°F, preferably with a daytime temperature rise of around 10°C/17°F.

Finding the right spot

Which room? Conservatory, kitchen, bathroom or living room? If plants are being grown on a windowsill, does it have curtains or blinds? Temperatures indoors tend to be relatively stable, but if the curtains are closed in the evening the windowsill can become very chilly. Especially during cold weather, it may be advisable to bring plants into the room overnight. Is there central heating? Rooms are traditionally kept at around 20°C/68°F in the daytime, but the room will be cooler overnight. Is there a radiator beneath the windowsill? If so, the atmosphere may be too dry. Both central heating and air conditioning dry the atmosphere. A room may also be too warm at night, and constant high temperatures can inhibit flowering (see moth orchid, page 104, and *Cymbidium*, page 63).

The aspect of a window is important. Generally speaking, a window that does not receive direct sunlight will not provide sufficient light. An east-facing aspect is often ideal, as plants receive the early morning sun and there is little danger of scorching the leaves. Likewise a west-facing window receives light later in the day, when the sun is lower in the sky. The midday summer sun in a sunny window is likely to cause the leaves to heat up and they can become scorched. Such windows should be lightly shaded. Net curtains provide a suitably dappled shade. Trees or shrubs planted close to the house in summer may provide increased shading.

Do not be afraid of moving plants from one room to another to find the right spot for each particular plant, but beware of moving any from low light to high light too quickly, as this can scorch the leaves. A red pigment in leaves is the plant's way of protecting itself from too much light. If leaves begin to acquire a slightly red hue this is a sign that light levels are on

Protecting furniture

To avoid water damage to furniture, set each pot on a ceramic or plastic dish – or place your plant pot in an attractive container. Glazed ceramic pots (which are, therefore, impermeable to water and have no holes in the base) are available with a rim inside designed to prevent the plant pot itself from sitting on the bottom of the ornamental pot. Any surplus water will be in the bottom of the pot, and so the chance of the compost being waterlogged is reduced. Alternatively, you may wish to use a simple glazed pot with no holes in the base. If the glazed pot is too large, one solution is to insert an empty plant pot upside-down in the glazed pot, so that the orchid plant in its container is at the required height.

Good companion plants for orchids
Members of the pineapple family, bromeliads, are found growing only in the Americas. They make good companion plants for orchids. There are two basic types: 'urn plants', which hold water in a central 'reservoir' and, besides being attractive in their own right, can be used to help maintain a humid environment around an orchid; and silvery leaved 'air plants', which require very little watering, and can be maintained by light spraying of rainwater.

Orchids also look good when grouped alongside other non-orchidaceous flowering and foliage plants such as ferns, begonias or areca palm (*Dypsis lutescens*) (see Companion planting on a windowsill, page 58, and Planting up a terrarium, page 116).

Moth orchids (*Phalaenopsis*) make ideal windowsill orchids. When grown in a sunny position, they should be given some shade in the middle of the day.

the borderline of becoming too high, and it may be advisable to provide a little more shading, or to move the plant to a place where light levels are a little lower.

Humidity
Central heating can produce a very dry atmosphere – something that orchids are likely to resent. Thus the key to successful home growing is often providing sufficient humidity. This can be achieved by standing potted plants in a tray containing water-retaining material such as expanded clay granules and by companion planting including non-orchidaceous plants (see box, left, and Companion planting on a windowsill, page 58). Terrariums are becoming an increasingly popular and attractive way of growing plants in the home (see Planting up a terrarium, page 116), and are a way of providing a suitably humid micro-environment.

Regularly misting your plants with rainwater will assist in maintaining humidity. However, you should never mist an orchid in full sunlight: in the middle of the day, for example.

Kitchen
The kitchen windowsill can be an excellent choice for growing many orchids. Not only is it relatively humid when compared to other rooms (apart from the bathroom), but the flowers can also be enjoyed while preparing a meal, and when washing up afterwards. It is also the place where you are most likely to carry out your repotting. If your kitchen is built as an extension on the back of the house, you may worry that

night-time temperatures may be too low. You need not. The lower evening temperatures can often be beneficial in promoting flowering in moth orchids (*Phalaenopsis*), for example.

Bathroom
Bathrooms are normally the most humid rooms in the house and, as such, can provide an ideal environment, provided there is appropriate light for the orchid in question.

Lounge/living room/dining room
These rooms may be the place you would most like to display your orchids. They are likely to be the warmest in the home, and possibly the driest. Such a room may be a temporary home, and plants that are no longer in flower can be moved to another room until they come into bloom once more.

Bedroom
Bedrooms tend to be cooler than living rooms. What could be better than a cool-growing orchid in full bloom to greet you when you wake up in the morning?

Conservatory
A conservatory can increase the range of orchids that can be grown in the home throughout the year, and can be ideal for plants such as standard-sized cymbidiums or sobralias, which are too large for other rooms. Because of the large expanses of glass (a good thing for maintaining light levels), the main danger for plants is that conservatories may be subject to temperature extremes. They can become too hot in summer, in which case you will need to introduce some sort of shading such as blinds or shade cloth (see Growing tropical orchids in a greenhouse: Temperature, below). Conversely, conservatories can become too cold in winter, in which case you should install a heater.

Basement or cellar
Orchids can also be grown successfully under artificial light in a basement or cellar, where you can provide a constant eighteen hours of light and six hours of darkness throughout the year.

GROWING TROPICAL ORCHIDS IN A GREENHOUSE

For anyone coming from a temperate climate, with its short winter's days often combined with icy weather, seeing orchids being grown in tropical and subtropical countries is liable to elicit pangs of jealousy. Plants that are strictly greenhouse subjects in temperate regions grow in gardens and under shade cloth in tropical and subtropical areas.

In cool-temperate regions a greenhouse provides an opportunity to grow a wide range of plants, and can be divided into sections, each with a different temperature regime. Learn what will grow in your greenhouse, rather than trying to grow everything under one set of conditions.

The three elements that you need to control in the greenhouse are temperature, light and humidity. Each will affect the other, and the trick is to achieve the right balance.

Temperature
The problem is generally more one of keeping temperatures down

The temptation is always to grow as many plants as possible in the greenhouse. Good air movement between plants is, however, essential.

Air movement

It is tempting to cram in as many plants as possible into a small space, but it is also important that air is allowed to circulate around the plants. Good air movement in the greenhouse with the aid of a fan helps to maintain an even temperature throughout. High leaf temperature can cause unsightly burning (see Finding the right spot, page 16). Moist stagnant air promotes fungal problems (see Diseases, page 137). Close packing of plants aids the spread of pests (see page 134).

(below 30°C/86°F) in summer than of providing sufficient heat in winter. Temperatures can increase rapidly when the sun comes out, leading to overheating. Greenhouses, therefore, normally require shading throughout summer, either with shade cloth or a white-reflective shading compound. Shade cloth is available in a range of values for percentage light reduction. To get the maximum benefit, suspend the cloth clear of the glass, to allow air movement between the shading and the greenhouse panels. Alternatively, apply shading compound early in the growing season, adding more coats as required. Remove shading in autumn, to let in more light when days are short and the sun is low in the sky. Aim for a day- and night-time temperature difference of at least 5°C/9°F.

To reduce heat loss (and keep heating bills down) most growers insulate their greenhouses with ultraviolet-stable, horticultural-grade bubble wrap, which traps air in small pockets. After three or four years, the bubble wrap will have deteriorated, become dirty and, in a humid greenhouse, become covered with green algae, and must be replaced.

Automatic ventilators in the apex of the greenhouse, which open at set temperatures to allow warm air to escape, unfortunately can lead to a loss of humidity. Bottom ventilators, set below the level of greenhouse staging, allow cooler air to be drawn in as the warmer air escapes through the top ventilators.

Hot-water pipes are ideal for heating a greenhouse, providing a gentle constant heat, but they are expensive to install. Today's orchid growers are much more likely to use an electric fan heater. Paraffin heaters that vent inside the greenhouse are not usually recommended as, among other potential problems, they can produce ethylene (ethene) gas, which causes bud drop.

Light

The application of shading inevitably reduces light levels (see Temperature, page 18). Nevertheless, the amount of available light will vary in different parts of the greenhouse, and plants should be placed in areas that mimic their natural habitats as far as possible (see the position information in each plant profile, pages 38–129). Cattleyas, for example, grow high in the canopy and are xerophytes, with tough leaves and a thick cuticle. They should be given as much light as possible, without scorching the leaves. A little reddening of leaves caused by the production of protective anthocyanins is acceptable. But if plants are too close to the glass, high leaf temperatures can lead to burning.

Those orchids that are adapted to the low light conditions of a cloud forest, such as restrepias, need more shade, and can be grown lower down, closer to the greenhouse floor (where it is also more humid), or placed under the staging, provided that it is not too dark.

Humidity

The atmosphere in an orchid house should have the delicious aroma of damp earth. Technically speaking, a relative humidity of around 80 per cent is optimum for most orchids.

The floor of the greenhouse and under the staging should be consistently moist. This can be achieved by regularly watering the greenhouse floor with a watering can, and filling trays with water. Pots can be placed on mesh above gravel-filled trays of water on the greenhouse staging. Some growers employ automatic spray systems or fog generators.

When will it flower?

The two main factors that affect flowering time are day length and temperature. Many orchid species are stimulated to flower by the shortening days of autumn, others by the lengthening days of spring. Cymbidiums and moth orchids (*Phalaenopsis*) need a fall in temperature to induce them to flower. In addition to the size of the plant, pseudobulbs of cattleyas need to reach a certain size threshold before the plant will bloom, while the foliage fans of paphiopedilums need to reach a critical length.

GROWING ORCHIDS IN A COLD GREENHOUSE OR COLD FRAME

A wide range of terrestrial orchids from temperate regions can be cultivated in an unheated greenhouse, or in a greenhouse with a minimum of heating that keeps temperatures above freezing. They include numerous plants from Mediterranean-type climates, plus some South African, Chilean and Australian

Moth orchids (*Phalaenopsis*) can be trained to produce lovely arching stems, giving a waterfall effect.

Enjoying plants from the greenhouse
Do bring your flowering greenhouse-grown plants into the home for a while, so that everyone can enjoy them. Or hang them outdoors on a veranda in a sheltered spot, to avoid damaging winds.

orchids. Many (but not all) can also be grown in the garden with some additional winter protection.

For such orchids ensure the greenhouse top and bottom ventilators are open as much as possible, to provide good air movement. Plants can be grown in a plunge bed within the greenhouse. This keeps the compost evenly moist, and the roots cool. Bury the pot (usually terracotta) in moist horticultural sand to just below the pot rim, with the top of the compost level with the sand.

Temperate orchids such as cypripediums will tolerate and even thrive in cold winters, and can be grown in pots in a cold frame. Indeed, the increasingly mild winters that are becoming more frequent in many countries may induce plants to start into growth too early in the season, and they require some protection against late frosts. They resent being both wet and cold, and need winter protection against the rain, at the same time as having good air movement around them.

GROWING ORCHIDS IN THE GARDEN
A wide range of hardy terrestrial orchids that are every bit as exotic as their tropical cousins can be grown in the garden in temperate regions. Provided that a few simple rules are

If you are extremely fortunate, orchids such as this green-winged orchid (*Anacamptis morio*) may appear in your lawn or mini-meadow.

Lawn management
It is not unusual to find wild orchids appearing in lawns. The key to maintaining orchids in the lawn lies in cutting the grass at the right times of the year – once after the orchids have flowered, and once after the seeds have been dispersed. After the grass has been mown, remove the cuttings. This will gradually reduce the lawn's fertility, because in lush, well-fertilized soil orchids are out-competed by more vigorous plants. Alternatively, it may be possible to mark the position of each orchid with a cane and later cut around individual orchid plants. See also Creating an orchid mini-meadow, page 44.

followed, they will thrive. Most garden soils, with a little modification perhaps, are suitable for growing orchids. It is, however, important that the soil has not been enriched with excessive nutrients, does not have a high organic matter content and is free-draining. If you have heavy clay soil, add horticultural grit to improve drainage. If you have very light soil, add some inorganic, water-retentive material such as clay granules.

A further option is to prepare a special orchid bed, and replace the soil with suitable compost (see Potting composts and soils, page 26). Bee orchids (*Ophrys apifera*), for example, prefer calcareous (>pH 7) soil.

Always plant your orchids well away from trees or shrubs, which remove moisture from the soil, so that it becomes too dry.

Orchids can make spectacular displays when grown in troughs, garden borders or in pockets of damp soil in alpine rock gardens, where rocks can shade the roots from excessive heat. Ferns, some of the smaller hostas, epimediums and small bulbs make suitable companion plants.

Different species and genera require different conditions: for example, showy orchid (*Cypripedium reginae*) and southern marsh orchid (*Dactylorhiza praetermissa*) are suitable for planting around a pond margin in full sun or dappled shade, where they can form large colonies. Cypripediums are typically woodland plants. They require several hours of sun in the early morning and the late evening. They should not be exposed to the midday summer sun, at which time they need dappled shade. If you want to move plants easily from one spot to another, grow them in large aquatic baskets that have numerous large holes.

CHOOSING AND BUYING ORCHIDS

If you are new to orchid growing, buy your first plants when they are in flower. Ideally, the flowers will have just opened and there will be unopened buds, although some popular orchids such as tropical slipper orchids (*Paphiopedilum* and *Phragmipedium*) usually only have a single flower. Consider how long the plant has been in flower. How long has it been on display? The presence of unopened buds is a sign that the flowers are not approaching the end of their lifespans. Yellowing buds are bad news. They may indicate that the plant has not been watered, or has been kept in a dry atmosphere. Such plants should be avoided. If there are a number of the same orchid for sale, pick up and examine them all, and select the best. You may find a plant with an additional flower spike that is just emerging. Choose vigorous, healthy-looking plants. Are the leaves nice and green and firm? Is the compost dry? If the orchid is growing in a clear pot, check that the roots are healthy (see Where do orchids grow?, pages 12–15). Look out for pests (see page 134).

If buying from a nursery, seek advice on how best to grow the plant. If you are buying a species, ask if it has been grown from seed (sadly, illegal wild-collected species are still sometimes offered for sale). It is surprising how quickly you can develop an eye for a good plant. Named varieties have been specifically selected for the quality of their blooms. They can be divisions of the parent plant, or have been produced in quantity by tissue culture to be genetically identical to the parent.

Your plant will need some protection while you take it home. A large fall in temperature can cause bud drop. Likewise you want to avoid temperatures that are too high, especially in summer, and in your car. Orchid nurseries usually wrap their sales carefully in tissue paper. Supermarkets and other outlets generally sell plants wrapped in plastic sleeves. Take care when unwrapping a plant; it may be preferable to cut the plastic sleeve open with scissors, rather than risk damaging the flowers.

Bare-root epiphytic orchids

Phytosanitary regulations for imported plants are designed to avoid the importation of exotic plant pests and diseases, thus imported plants are often offered for sale by foreign nurseries that are bare root, and probably wrapped in moist sphagnum moss. The danger is that such plants may quickly become desiccated. Likewise, you may be offered a division of a particularly desirable clone (of a cattleya, for example) that has little or no root. Before planting, rehydrate the plant, by soaking the base for a number of hours in a bucket of water.

Expanding your hobby
The orchid-growing community is large and friendly. Joining your local orchid society enables you to swap stories with like-minded people and to learn more about cultivation from more experienced growers. Societies also put on local shows, where you can enjoy seeing and purchasing a wider range of orchid species and hybrids than are normally available for sale at local garden centres. Nursery people are always more than willing to offer advice on how best to grow your purchases. Larger national and international shows attract nurseries from a wide range of countries, further widening the choice of plants available to the hobbyist grower.

Orchid seedlings
Buying small seedlings is a relatively inexpensive way of increasing your orchid collection. Part of the excitement of buying seedlings is their genetic variability: no two seedlings will be exactly alike. There is always the possibility that one of your seedlings will turn out to be a real prizewinner. Of course, there is also the possibility that the offspring could be inferior to the parent plants. If you are buying species orchids, in all likelihood they will be more like their parents than if you are buying hybrid seedlings. The disadvantage of buying seedlings is that it may be some years before they flower. But think of the excitement of seeing the buds develop as they come into flower for the first time.

Often orchid seedlings benefit from being grown on in a propagator, which will maintain a humid environment. It can be placed on a shady windowsill, perhaps with a little bottom heat. Keep compost moist, feed regularly with dilute fertilizer and repot frequently into a fine-grade compost (see Potting composts and soils, page 26). Seedlings with pseudobulbs should become progressively larger each year (see Orchid growth patterns, page 13). As you become more expert, you may consider buying flasks of seedlings (see Growing tropical orchids from a flask of seedlings, page 50).

EQUIPMENT

Pots and containers
Terracotta or plastic? Each has its advantages and disadvantages, and it is often a matter of personal preference. Plants dry out more quickly in terracotta pots, and need to be watered more frequently. Plastic pots are lighter than terracotta and retain moisture for longer, but it is easier to overwater. Choose a pot with sufficient drainage. You can sometimes find specially made clay orchid pots with extra drainage holes. Additional drainage holes can easily be cut in plastic pots. Aquarium pots have many large holes but may need to be lined, with sphagnum moss for example, to prevent loss of compost. Some growers like to use clear plastic pots, allowing them to see the roots.

Some orchids, such as vandas, either resent their roots being confined to a pot, or have a scrambling habit that

Some growers prefer to use terracotta pots. Orchid pots, with their extra holes, provide rapid drainage.

makes them difficult, if not impossible, to grow in pots. Plants with pendulous flower spikes, such as *Brassavola perrinii* or many of the *Dendrobium* species with pendulous canes, are normally better grown in baskets (see Growing orchids in a basket, page 84) or mounted on a piece of bark or a tree-fern slab (see Mounting orchids on bark, page 94). The roots will be free to scramble over the surface of the mount, to which they may adhere, or dangle free in the air, according to their nature. Plants that have been mounted dry out much more quickly than those grown in pots, and normally require daily watering or misting.

Other essentials

- water butt – for collecting rainwater
- watering can (with a long, thin spout) – for reaching plants at the rear of the greenhouse staging
- mister spray – a small, hand-held mister can be used to mist leaves of plants in the home (but beware of leaving water in the crowns of plants); a larger garden spray can be used in a greenhouse
- canes of various sizes – for training flower stems
- rubber or plastic cane protectors – for the tops of canes to provide eye protection; such caps are essential
- clips, raffia or soft string – for tying and training flower stems as they develop
- pest control kit – for tackling any symptoms of pests or diseases (see Troubleshooting, page 134)
- secateurs, scissors or knives – for trimming damaged leaves
- dishes or trays – for standing pots on, on a windowsill

Glass jars

Vanda hybrids have a monopodial habit (see Orchid growth patterns, page 13), with large fans of dark green leaves and magnificent flowers in an array of rich colours from the deepest indigo to a vibrant pink. They can be grown in the home in tall glass jars. Fill the jar containing the orchid with water or a dilute solution of fertilizer that has been allowed to reach room temperature; leave for about an hour, to enable the thick white roots to absorb the moisture. Pour the remaining water out of the vase, leaving the plant enclosed in a suitably humid environment.

- gravel or expanded clay granules – for placing in a tray to increase humidity around the plants
- soft cloth – for wiping dust from leaves

Useful extras

- compost bins – for storing different compost components
- propagator – for seedlings; a heated propagator is an invaluable addition for growing seedlings
- galvanized, plastic-coated wire or fishing line – for mounting orchids
- bradawl – for making holes in cork-bark mounts
- scalpel with disposable blades (for vegetative propagation)
- tools for seed sowing: forceps (tweezers), scissors, stapler, glass jars (or Petri dishes), unbleached coffee filter paper, porridge oats, agar, pressure cooker or microwave (see Growing a dactylorhiza from seed, page 72)

Caring for your equipment

All pots, other containers and tools must be thoroughly cleaned after use. To prevent the spread of diseases, either sterilize cutting tools by flaming after dipping in alcohol, or by using a blowtorch, or a solution of disinfectant. But bear in mind that leaving metal tools in disinfectant solutions can lead to the tools becoming corroded.

Sharpen scissors, knives and secateurs regularly, and oil them. Clean greenhouse glass to maximize the amount of light, particularly in winter.

POTTING COMPOSTS AND SOILS

It sometimes seems that every orchid grower has his or her favourite mix.

An open mixture of bark, sphagnum moss and perlite is water-retentive while allowing for plenty of air around the roots.

These can change over time, often according to availability. Do not be a 'fashion victim'. The aim always is to provide a compost that is well-aerated but still retains sufficient moisture for that plant's needs. The one thing all composts have in common is that, before use, they must always be moistened by soaking overnight in a bucket of water.

You can purchase bags of pre-made orchid mixes from orchid nurseries and garden centres, but you may prefer to make your own, or to modify the compost you have bought.

Composts for epiphytes and tropical terrestrials

- *Bark* sold as being suitable for growing orchids is usually composed of different species of pine (*Pinus*) trees, and can vary in quality. Never use bark sold for use on paths or as a mulch. Pine bark breaks down slowly, and can last a number of years without having to be replaced. It is available in various grades. As a rough guide, the smallest size (6–9mm/¼–⅜in diameter) is suitable for seedlings or orchids with fine roots, such as masdevallias and oncidiums. Medium grade (9–12mm/⅜–½in diameter) is suitable for paphiopedilums, for example. The largest size of bark pieces (12–18mm/½–¾in diameter) is appropriate for growing adult plants with thick roots such as cymbidiums or sobralias.
- *Charcoal* is sometimes found in potting compost to keep the medium 'sweet', meaning that it has the ability to absorb undesirable salts, for example.
- *Coconut fibre* is the outer husk of a coconut. It has good water-retaining qualities, and is often incorporated into seedling composts. It does, however, break down relatively rapidly, and should be replaced more frequently than bark.
- *Peat* is still used by some nurseries in their composts (particularly for cymbidiums) despite there being concerns regarding its sustainability.
- *Perlite* is an expanded volcanic glass. It is very light and retains a lot of air. It should be moistened before use. Wear a dust mask to avoid inhaling any fine particles.
- *Rock wool,* comprising a mixture of absorbent and non-absorbent fibrous materials, is still occasionally encountered and can be an excellent medium for South American slipper orchids (*Phragmipedium*), for example. As rock wool is entirely devoid of nutrients, this is a hydroponic medium, and nutrients are supplied as a dilute fertilizer. Some people are allergic to the fine fibres in rock wool, and it may be advisable to wear a mask and gloves when handling this medium.
- *Sphagnum moss* takes up and retains large amounts of water. Ensure your source is harvested sustainably. If your orchid is growing in sphagnum alone, replace it annually.
- *Other additions* to potting composts can include small cubes of artificial sponge, which are designed to retain moisture, or cork granules.

Soil and potting composts for temperate/hardy orchids

As a general rule, temperate orchids need soil or compost that is moisture-retentive but has good drainage. Traditionally, both clay and sandy soils can be improved by adding organic material such as garden compost. Drainage in heavy clay soil can also be improved by adding pumice, perlite or coarse horticultural sand (not builders' sand). Avoid using peat; it tends to retain too much moisture, and removal of peat is generally environmentally damaging.

A good-quality loam is the backbone of many terrestrial compost mixes. It is a soil that contains a mixture of different sizes of soil particles and adequate humus (organic matter). It has a crumb structure that allows for plenty of air to circulate around the roots, and provides good drainage.

Useful additions for composts or soil for terrestrial orchids

- *Blood fish and bone* or *bonemeal* can be incorporated sparingly into garden soil as a slow-release fertilizer. It should be handled with gloves to avoid the risk of infection by salmonella.
- *Composted pine bark* can make a useful water-retentive addition.
- *Good-quality garden loam* – ophrys needs loam that is neutral to slightly alkaline (>pH 7).
- *Horticultural grit* with a diameter of 2–4mm/1⁄16–1⁄8in.
- *Horticultural sand* to enhance soil drainage; never add builders' sand, as it is too alkaline.
- *Leafmould* is an ideal alternative to peat for improving soil structure, or as an addition to potting composts. Make this by finely chopping moist leaves of oak (*Quercus*) or beech (*Fagus*). Avoid leaves of evergreens, sycamore (*Acer pseudoplatanus*) and horse chestnut (*Aesculus*). Place the prepared leaves in a black plastic bag aerated by a few holes and store for one or two years, to allow the leaves to break down. Sieve before use.
- *Pumice* comprises large pieces of frothy lava that hold water and improve drainage.

HOW TO PLANT GARDEN ORCHIDS

Orchids can be planted in the garden in spring or autumn, depending on the genus. Plant dactylorhizas in the open ground in spring as the foliage begins to emerge, and after the last frosts (otherwise protect them with cloches, for example). Some time before planting, water each container-grown plant well. The compost should be moist, but not sopping wet. Remove any other plants such as liverworts from the surface of the compost. Dig a hole the same size as the pot, and pour water into the bottom of the hole. Remove the orchid carefully from its pot, taking care not to damage the tubers, and place in the hole, together with the compost from the container. Gently firm the soil around the plant and water. Label the plant and then protect it by covering with a wire cage until it becomes established.

Temperate slipper orchids (*Cypripedium*) are best planted in autumn, giving the roots time to grow, and the plants time to become established before winter. Excavate a saucer-shaped depression, with a diameter a little larger than that of the root system, leaving a small mound in the middle. Place the plant on top of the mound, and arrange the roots carefully in a fan around the central shoot(s). Replace the soil, with the shoot(s) just below the surface. Erect some winter protection such as a cloche over the plant. It is not the cold that is the killer – many temperate slipper orchids grow in mountainous areas, where temperatures regularly fall well below freezing throughout winter, but there they are protected by an insulating covering of snow. It is the cold combined with the wet that is the problem for these plants.

Southern marsh orchid (*Dactylorhiza praetermissa*) requires more moisture. It can be planted around pond margins.

The attractively patterned leaves of the common spotted orchid (*Dactylorhiza fuchsii*) appear above ground in spring.

WATERING

That more plants die in cultivation from overwatering than underwatering applies equally to orchids. There are, unfortunately, no hard-and-fast rules as to when a plant requires watering. It depends to an extent on the environmental conditions under which it is being grown. Generally speaking, you should water plants when the compost has dried out (but it should not be allowed to become bone dry, making re-wetting of the compost difficult, if not impossible). Water when roots are actively growing, otherwise the compost should be damp or moist rather than wet.

Water type and its temperature

Always use rainwater if at all possible. Depending on your water supply, tap water can be substituted occasionally. Water quality is more of a problem if you live in a hard- rather than a soft-water area, because hard water contains a high level of salts. Repeated spraying with hard water will cause a white deposit on the surfaces of leaves. A build-up of salts in the compost will cause roots to die.

Drinking water is normally chlorinated at the treatment plant to kill any potential pathogens. If using tap water, allow the water to stand in a container overnight, allowing the chlorine to evaporate. To avoid giving plants a cold shock, ensure the water temperature is similar to that in the room or greenhouse.

When to water

Depending on what you are growing, as a rough guideline water plants in pots once a week: more often in summer perhaps, if the weather has been unusually hot; less frequently in winter. Have the rainwater that you have saved ready at room temperature. Ideally, water early in the morning, as the temperature begins to rise, allowing excess water on surfaces to evaporate, and before there is any possibility of the sun burning the leaves.

Water according to the weather. Especially where plants are being cultivated in a greenhouse or the garden, orchid growers are avid watchers of the daily weather forecast. Watering is best carried out on warm sunny mornings. There will be less of a need to water on overcast days.

Although you can water your plants later in the day, avoid leaving water in the shoots and crowns of plants; as the temperature falls in the evenings, fungal

Where possible, orchids should be watered with rainwater, which can be collected in a water butt.

and bacterial spores can germinate in the moisture and lead to rotting of new shoots.

How to water

When watering a plant in a pot, always water thoroughly, allowing water to run copiously out through the bottom of the pot. Get into the habit of picking up your pots before and after watering. A pot that needs watering will feel lighter than one that has just been watered. In the house, allow pots to drain on the draining board or in the sink, before returning them to their allocated homes.

When replacing the plant, you may want to keep the plant in the same orientation as prior to watering. This can be important if the plant is developing a flower spike, which may be drawn towards the light.

Spray roots that are growing outside the pot until they turn green. If plants are being grown on a mount (see Mounting orchids on bark, page 94), you may choose to immerse the whole plant (but not any flowers) in a container of water or diluted feed at the ambient temperature.

If the pseudobulbs are showing signs of shrivelling, or the leaves appear limp and wrinkled, examine the plant's roots. The problem could be overwatering or underwatering. Overwatering can result in wet, soggy compost; underwatered potting compost will be very dry and can be difficult to re-wet. It is pointless watering dead roots.

FEEDING

Epiphytic orchids

Epiphytes exist on a dilute soup of nutrients. Rainwater contains small amounts of nitrates from lightning, and carbonic acid from dissolved carbon dioxide. Orchids are just one component of a plant community, growing alongside mosses, lichens and other plants that often form thick humus mats of decaying vegetation enriched by animal droppings. Compared with many other plants, orchids tend to be slow growers, and it is generally advisable to feed them with half-strength, or sometimes one-quarter strength, fertilizer.

A high-nitrogen feed is generally recommended during the growing period, and a high-potash one towards the end of the growing period, to encourage 'harder' leaves and to stimulate flowering. Specialist orchid fertilizers are available, and should be used according the the manufacturer's instructions.

Include fertilizer in the watering regime only when plants are actively growing. Any build-up of salts in the potting compost must be avoided, because it can lead to the death of the roots – and eventually the plant. Therefore, water plants copiously with just rainwater every third or fourth watering.

Terrestrial orchids

Terrestrial orchids generally originate in low-nutrient habitats and should be grown in soil to which artificial fertilizers have not been applied (see Growing orchids in the garden, page 21). They may respond to the occasional application of an extremely weak, balanced fertilizer when grown in pots, but be very circumspect. If in doubt, do not feed.

TRAINING FLOWER STEMS

Whereas orchids may produce single flowers on short stems, many of the popular genera such as *Phalaenopsis* carry their flowers on long, and sometimes branching, stems. Their flower spikes will grow towards the light source, especially where plants are growing on a windowsill. You can either maintain plants in the same orientation, or else turn them regularly to avoid wiggly stems.

To display the orchid flowers to their best advantage, either for a show or for your own personal enjoyment, the stems of many orchids benefit from being tied to a suitable supporting cane, which should be hidden as far as possible (see Training flower spikes, page 102).

Because their flower spikes emerge from the base of the plant and proceed to grow downwards, so that they dangle beneath the parent plant, orchids such as stanhopeas are more suitable for mounting (see Mounting orchids on bark, page 94) or growing in a basket (see Growing orchids in a basket, page 84.

CLEANING

In the home (and greenhouse) wipe both surfaces of leaves with a leaf shine or water once a month, using a clean damp cloth or tissue and ensuring that the leaves are dry when you have finished. Removing grime allows more light to reach the plant tissues, essential for photosynthesis.

Watch out
Garden canes can be a safety hazard, especially to eyes when bending over to examine a plant. They should, therefore, be topped with protective rubber or plastic caps.

Your plants will benefit from regular cleaning of their leaves, with a damp cloth or tissue. Then wipe them dry.

Good greenhouse hygiene is essential. Sweep the floor regularly to ensure it is clear of plant debris. Pay particular attention to plants at the rear of the staging, and in hard-to-reach corners where pests can lurk without being detected for long periods, and serious infestations build up.

Remove any debris from the vicinity of a greenhouse, or indeed in the garden. Do not give slugs and snails somewhere to hide. Woodlice thrive beneath decaying vegetation.

Before reuse, scrub pots thoroughly using a detergent, to prevent the spread of pests (particularly tiny slugs) and diseases. Rinse well with clean water.

REPOTTING

Looking after your plant's root system is one of the keys to successful orchid growing. A healthy root system is necessary to support the rest of the plant. The function of roots is to anchor the plant to the substrate, and to take up water and nutrients. In common with other plant parts, roots need oxygen to 'breathe', and a waterlogged growing medium will rapidly lead to their death, and eventually that of the whole plant. This is especially true of epiphytic species, where so-called air roots may be seen dangling in the humid atmosphere, and should not be confined to a pot.

As a general rule, plants grown in pots will benefit from regular repotting. Certainly, it is always a mistake to wait until the compost has broken down. If unsure, do not be afraid to tap the plant out of its pot and examine the root system and compost. The compost should smell 'sweet' and not form a soggy mass.

If an orchid has become pot-bound, it may be time to move it to a larger container. However, if many of the roots are dead, they should be cut away, leaving only sufficient roots to anchor the plant. In this case, a smaller pot may be required.

Epiphytic orchids

If a plant is doing well in a particular compost, stick with it. Examine the compost carefully, to see exactly what

Looking after your moth orchid once flowered

When a moth orchid (*Phalaenopsis*) has finished flowering there are two options: cut off the flower spike close to its base; or, if the plant is robust, cut it at a point two or three nodes up from the base. In the latter case, a new branch may grow and flower.

Repot moth orchids in spring, as temperatures and light levels increase and the thick, silvery roots produce bright green or reddish tips and resume growing. Because they are epiphytes, they are feeling at home if the roots are growing out of the pot and into the humid air.

At least every two years, and sooner if there are signs that the compost is beginning to break down, repot a moth orchid. It is always a mistake to wait until the plant shows signs of distress, such as the leaves becoming floppy (wilting) before taking any action. The plant should be repotted immediately. If you are unsure, do not be afraid to remove the plant gently from its pot. The root ball should remain intact. The compost should not be a wet and soggy mass.

Moth orchids are often sold in clear pots, allowing you to see both the roots and the state of the compost. It is a common myth that these plants need to be repotted in a clear pot. While it is true that, when wet, the roots turn green and can photosynthesize, when compared with that made by the leaves the contribution of the roots to the plant's nutrition is minimal.

It is a mistake to repot in too large a container. If there is not a healthy root system after pruning the roots, you may need to use a smaller pot than previously.

Purchase suitable orchid compost from a garden centre or nursery. Alternatively, pot plants in medium- to coarse-grade orchid bark, with the addition, if preferred, of some chopped sphagnum moss. After repotting, a moth orchid will benefit from daily spraying; take care not to allow water to remain in the crown of the plant.

Once your orchid has finished flowering, you have a choice. You can either cut the flower spike close to the base (left), and wait for another flowering shoot to appear; or you can cut the spike just above a node (right), in which case a new flowering shoot may develop from that node.

the orchid is growing in. It could be peat, bark or coconut fibre (see Potting composts and soils, page 26). It may contain small pieces of sponge, or lumps of charcoal. It could be speckled with perlite. It could be almost any combination of these.

If it is not your usual orchid compost, you may be tempted to take the plant out of its pot and repot in your own compost. However, should the plant be growing well, the best advice is probably to wait until the usual potting time in the following spring to decide whether or not to repot. Once you are ready to repot an orchid, follow the instructions in Repotting a cymbidium (see page 64).

Do not overpot, because this can prevent the compost from drying out, and lead to the death of those all-important roots. Choose a container that fits the size of the root ball, leaving sufficient space for new growth. Especially if the root system is poor, it is sometimes preferable to repot in a smaller pot than previously.

Terrestrial orchids

The underground structures vary considerably (see individual plant profiles, pages 38–129): for example, whereas dactylorhizas have tubers that resemble small dahlia tubers, cypripediums form a mat of thin, branching roots.

Summergreen orchids (those whose foliage dies down in winter) should be repotted in fresh compost annually, in spring (see Repotting a cypripedium, page 68). For bletillas, calanthes, dactylorhizas and cypripediums do this as soon as the new shoots begin to appear. After storing them somewhere cool and dry over the summer months, repot tubers of wintergreen orchids (those that die down over summer), such as ophrys and pterostylis, in fresh compost in autumn as their new shoots begin to emerge.

The dramatic flowers of *Dracula vampira* emerge from the base of the plant. Such palnts are best grown in baskets.

HOLIDAY CARE

In the home

Orchids are tough, and probably survive better on a little benign neglect than their non-orchidaceous relatives. If you are going away for less than a week, water plants thoroughly and move them to a cool, shady spot. For longer spells, you might want to ask a friend to look after your plants. Although you do not want your plants to die from lack of moisture, neither do you want them to be overwatered. Leave your friends with clear instructions.

In the greenhouse

Depending on the time of year, leaving your greenhouse while you

Sowing disas
Disas are unusual in the orchid world in that they can be successfully raised from seed without using laboratory techniques. Sow on moist sphagnum moss in a propagator placed in the shade at room temperature (21°C/70°F). Once the seeds have germinated, they can be pricked out into small pots and grown on (see plant profile, page 79).

go away is asking a lot more of your friend. Therefore, you may need to give additional instructions on watering and spraying, damping down the greenhouse floor and opening and closing vents. If there are not too many, label individual plants with specific instructions, or group together plants with similar cultural requirements. One option for more tender orchids may be to move them temporarily into the home, to somewhere shady and cool.

In the garden
Ask your friend to water your plants if there is a hot dry spell.

PROPAGATION BY SOWING

Orchid seeds are tiny, the embryo sometimes consisting of as few as one hundred cells, with a seed coat as little as 0.11mm/0.004in long and weighing less than 0.5mg. As they are lacking any significant food reserve, to germinate in their natural habitats seeds must form a dangerous liaison with a suitable fungus. Although initially described as a symbiotic relationship, that is one where both partners benefit, more recently it has become clear that the relationship may be more one-sided – the orchid being the major beneficiary. Therefore, it is an example of mycotrophy (fungus eating). This dependence on a fungal partner (or series of fungal partners) can last a lifetime. For example, the toffee-coloured European bird's nest orchid (*Neottia nidus-avis*) does not produce any chlorophyll, and is entirely dependent on its woodland fungal partner(s). Indeed, it is only comparatively recently that scientists have come to appreciate that many plants, including probably most trees, form mutual relationships with soil fungi, and that there is a 'wood wide web' of fungi.

In the late nineteenth century some horticulturalists successfully germinated orchid seeds on the compost where adult orchid plants were growing. However, very few seedlings were obtained and, as soon as scientists developed a better understanding of the role of the fungus, techniques for germinating orchid seeds under laboratory conditions were developed. Today, the so-called symbiotic technique is used for some terrestrial orchids. Seeds of the green-winged orchid (*Anacamptis morio*) and many *Dactylorhiza* species will germinate relatively easily on a simple medium consisting of powdered porridge oats plus agar as a setting agent, to which a compatible fungus is added (see Growing a dactylorhiza from seed, page 72).

In addition, back in the 1920s, it became apparent that it was possible to germinate the seeds of the majority of orchids without the intervention of a fungus. Today, tropical orchids (and the majority of hardy orchids) are germinated asymbiotically (that is, without the aid of a fungus) on a sterile agar-jelly-based medium containing a mixture of nutrients that essentially replaces the role of the fungus. Although this is performed commercially under laboratory conditions, it is possible for the amateur grower to adopt the same technique using simple kitchen equipment. Flasks of seedlings are raised under artificial lighting, at around room temperature (21°C/70°F) until they are large enough to be transplanted into compost (see Growing tropical orchids from a flask of seedlings, page 50).

VEGETATIVE PROPAGATION

In addition to being grown from seed, many orchids can be propagated vegetatively by one of the methods described below. The offspring will be genetically identical to the parent plant.

To avoid potentially spreading plant diseases such as viruses and bacterial infections, sterilize all cutting tools between propagating each plant. This can be done by heating with a propane flame or using alcohol or a strong disinfectant solution; or by using a new scalpel blade each time. To reduce the chances of subsequent infection, allow cut surfaces to dry out.

Keikis

Some orchids occasionally produce new plantlets instead of flowers. These are referred to as keikis (said to be derived from the Hawaiian word for child). They can appear on canes of many species of *Dendrobium* when, instead of the expected flower, a bud develops as a shoot. Similarly, a bud on the flowering stem of a moth orchid (*Phalaenopsis*) will sometimes produce a keiki instead of a flower. Restrepias often produce keikis, in the axils of shoots.

To allow the keikis to further develop a good root system it may be helpful to wrap the developing roots in a moist sphagnum blanket held in place within a clear plastic wrapper. Once a strong root system has developed carefully remove the keiki from the parent plant, and pot in equal parts sphagnum moss and perlite.

Backbulbs

After dividing a cymbidium plant, you may be left with some plump green pseudobulbs that were at the rear of the plant. Often these backbulbs can be propagated by placing them in a sealed plastic bag with a little damp sphagnum moss, and leaving them until they produce new shoots. Pot up them in equal parts sphagnum moss and perlite (see Repotting a cymbidium, page 64).

Division

Instead of producing one shoot, sympodial orchids (see Orchid growth patterns, page 13), particularly if growing vigorously, can produce two or more 'leads'. Over a number of growing seasons, a large plant will result, and it can be divided into a number of

A well-grown noble orchid (*Dendrobium nobile*) will flower from every node, providing it is given a cool winter rest.

smaller sections. Do this by cutting the rhizome(s) so that, in addition to the main shoot, there are at least three strong pseudobulbs attached. Pot up each section (see Repotting a cymbidium, page 64).

Cuttings

It is not usually possible to propagate orchids by taking cuttings, but the following are useful exceptions.

As the shoots of jewel orchid (*Ludisia discolor*) lengthen, the lower leaves become dry and die. Choose a growth that will allow you to produce a shoot that is around 12cm/5in long, and make a cut straight across just below a node. This can be done at any time of the year, as long as the plant is actively growing. To induce rooting, immerse the cut end in a jar of water until roots develop, or else place directly into moist compost or sphagnum moss in a shady spot at room temperature (21°C/70°F). The cuttings should root rapidly. Once a good root system is established, pot the new plant in equal parts medium-grade bark, sphagnum moss and perlite.

Vanilla orchids are similarly easily propagated by taking stem cuttings. In spring, cut off a section of stem containing three or four nodes beginning to develop roots. Place on a bed of moist sphagnum moss in a propagator at room temperature (21°C/70°F) in the shade. Once the plants have developed a good root system, pot in pine-bark compost (see plant profile, page 128).

In spring, leafless stems (usually referred to as canes) of some *Dendrobium* species (*D. nobile*, for example) can be used to produce new plants by cutting them into sections that include three or four nodes. Place the cuttings on a bed of moist sphagnum moss in a propagator at room temperature (21°C/70°F) in the shade. Shoots will sprout from some of the nodes. Pot up the little plants once they have good root systems, into medium-grade bark.

In addition to producing keikis, restrepias can be propagated by taking leaf cuttings at any time of the year. Cut the stem of a leaf once the plant has already flowered. Press the cut surface into a small pot of sphagnum moss, up to the leaf base. Keep in cool shade (minimum temperature of 10°C/50°F), alongside its parent (see plant profile, page 114). Water regularly or mist to keep the moss moist. New leaves and roots will begin to develop after a few weeks.

Plants

Angraecum magdalenae

Height and spread	15x30cm/6x12in
Position	13–24°C/55–75°F
Position	Light summer shade
Flowering time	Summer

Large, beautiful, long-lasting, ivory flowers emerge on a short spike from a compact fan of leathery, grey-green leaves. This Madagascan species emits a spicy, slightly overpowering fragrance that fills the greenhouse in the evenings. The flowers are moth-pollinated.

—

WHERE TO GROW

Tolerates full sunlight, although some shading is recommended in the height of summer, to avoid leaf burn. Grow in an intermediate greenhouse.

HOW TO GROW

In its natural habitat, *A. magdalenae* grows in pockets of humus between large boulders, and is subject to a prolonged summer dry season. Pot in a mixture of equal parts medium-grade pine bark, leafmould and sphagnum moss. The compost mixture should remain moist.

GROWING TIP

Slugs and snails are attracted to the strongly perfumed flowers. Suitable countermeasures include setting beer traps, or moving *A. magdalenae* into the house to enjoy the flowers.

OTHER NOTABLE SPECIES

Angraecum sesquipedale (comet orchid) is also from Madagascar. Charles Darwin famously predicted that it would be pollinated by a moth with a tongue (proboscis) sufficiently long to reach the nectar at the base of its 30cm/12in floral spur. A much larger plant, its height and spread are 45x60cm/18x24in – and more in older specimens.

Tulip orchid

Anguloa clowesii aka Cradle orchid

The tulip orchid grows in woodland in Colombia and Venezuela. Flowers resembling large golden goblets that emit a delicious perfume of cinnamon and oil of wintergreen emerge from the base of the pseudobulb in spring, along with the new growths. This orchid can eventually become a very large specimen, with long, ribbed, plicate leaves.

—

Height and spread
70x30cm/27x12in

Temperature
10–24°C/50–75°F

Position
Dappled shade

Flowering time
Early summer

WHERE TO GROW

Cultivate in a cool to intermediate greenhouse, with a humid atmosphere. Provide summer shade and ensure there is good air movement.

HOW TO GROW

Plant in a free-draining mixture of equal parts fine pine bark, perlite and sphagnum moss. Water copiously throughout the growing season. Feed with one-quarter strength balanced fertilizer, flushing the compost through with rainwater every fourth watering. After the leaves have been shed in autumn, stop watering. Give the plant a winter rest without allowing the compost to dry excessively.

GROWING TIP

Prone to red spider mites infestations, so check the undersides of the leaves regularly (see Pests, page 134).

BY ANY OTHER NAME
The tiny mobile lip nestling in the centre of the tulip orchid flower rocks back and forth like a baby in its cradle – hence its alternative common name of cradle orchid.

Barkeria spectabilis

Height and spread	25x15cm/10x6in
Temperature	13–24°C/55–75°F
Position	Light summer shade
Flowering time	Summer

Long, thin, tapering, branching pseudobulbs produce up to twelve, long-lasting, rose-purple flowers, 7cm/3in across, each with spreading petals and sepals, and a white lip sprinkled with purple dots. The erect raceme emerges close to the apex of each mature pseudobulb.

—

WHERE TO GROW

Grow in a cool or intermediate greenhouse, or on a windowsill. In the greenhouse *B. spectabilis* can be positioned high in the greenhouse apex, but it needs sufficient shading to prevent the leaves burning.

HOW TO GROW

In its natural habitat in Mexico and Central America this orchid grows in the company of air plants (*Tillandsia* spp.) on thin oak branches. The roots resent being confined. Therefore, grow mounted on a section of branch (see Mounting orchids on bark, page 94).

GROWING TIP

Barkeria spectabilis is deciduous. Once the leaves have been shed in autumn, reduce watering. This orchid cannot tolerate being wet, and the compost must have dried out by each evening.

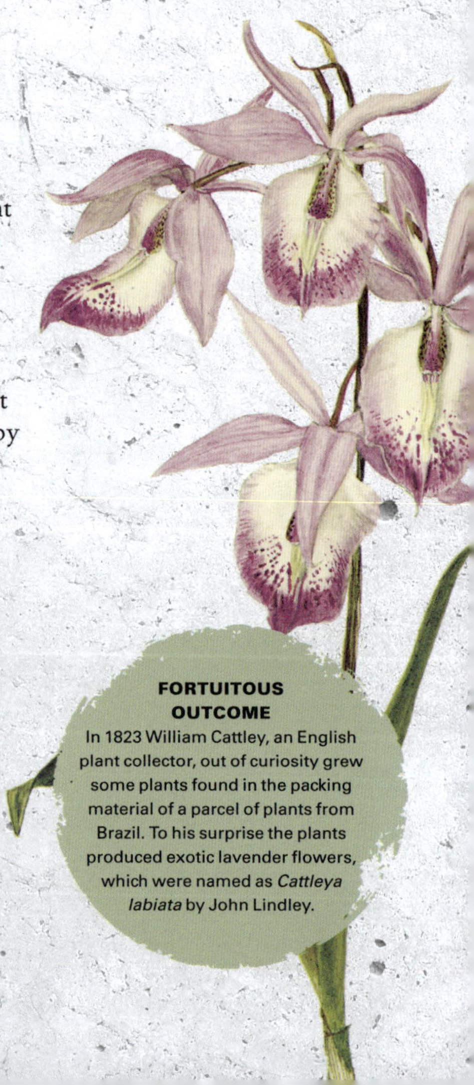

FORTUITOUS OUTCOME

In 1823 William Cattley, an English plant collector, out of curiosity grew some plants found in the packing material of a parcel of plants from Brazil. To his surprise the plants produced exotic lavender flowers, which were named as *Cattleya labiata* by John Lindley.

Hyacinth orchid

Bletilla striata

This lovely deciduous orchid from China and Japan is commonly called hyacinth orchid because of its pleasant fragrance, emitted by its sprays of small, prettily marked, purple flowers in early summer. Narrow, pleated leaves follow the flowers. Hybridizers have recently bred a range of colour varieties, with white, pale blue or pink flowers.

—

Height and spread
25x30cm/10x12in

Temperature
–10–24°C/14–75°F

Position
Full sun to light shade

Flowering time
Summer

WHERE TO GROW

Being a plant originating in cool regions, hyacinth orchid is hardy outdoors in temperate zones unless winter temperatures are very low. Grow in the garden, or in pots in a cold frame or cold greenhouse.

HOW TO GROW

If growing in pots, use a mixture with equal parts of loam (John Innes No. 2 in the UK) and perlite or horticultural grit. When planted in the garden, hyacinth orchid requires moist but well-drained soil, which, depending on the soil type, may benefit from the addition of organic material. It appreciates some shade during the hottest part of the day.

GROWING TIP

Plant hyacinth orchid's diminutive rhizomes, which resemble those of irises, just below the soil surface.

A MEDICINAL PLANT
Thought to have antioxidant and antimicrobial properties (among others), hyacinth orchid is becoming increasingly rare in the wild because of collection for traditional Chinese medicine.

Creating an orchid mini-meadow

When walking through a flower-rich meadow in full bloom in the early morning in late spring and summer it is easy to imagine you are in paradise. The enormous range of plant species hosted there means such a meadow is a hotspot of biodiversity. What could be better than establishing your own mini-meadow in your garden? Whatever its size, in addition to the pleasure it will bring, it will create a wildlife haven for many insects and other creatures.

Although many orchid-rich alpine meadows remain in Europe, sadly the native meadows of North America are largely a distant memory, having been ploughed and built on by the early settlers. The UK has lost an astonishing 93 per cent of these flower-rich meadows since the 1930s, mainly because of changes in agricultural practice. However, in 2013, green hay from flower-rich donor meadows was strewn widely by the Coronation Meadows Project in the UK, in order to establish a new meadow in every county to celebrate the sixtieth anniversary of the coronation of Queen Elizabeth II.

With the current revival of interest in creating more natural landscapes and gardens, many people would now like to establish their own mini-meadows, incorporating some orchids. For a perennial mini-meadow, it is important to purchase a perennial (not annual) seed mix, preferably of native species including yellow rattle (*Rhinanthus minor*). The aim is to reduce the vigour of grasses, and yellow rattle is a hemiparasite of grasses. Depending on the grass length, either cut it with shears or mow the mini-meadow in autumn. Remove and compost the cuttings. Once the mini-meadow is established, after one or two years, orchids can be introduced as plug plants in spring. The key to success in maintaining such a meadow lies in ensuring low soil fertility by cutting the herbage in autumn and then removing the cut material.

EUROPEAN ORCHIDS FOR A MINI-MEADOW

Autumn lady's tresses (*Spiranthes spiralis*)
Bee orchid (*Ophrys apifera*)
Common spotted orchid (*Dactylorhiza fuchsii*)
Green-winged orchid (*Anacamptis morio*)
Southern marsh orchid (*Dactylorhiza praetermissa*)

1 Orchids (here common spotted orchid) can be planted in a grassy area, but it is important to keep nutrient levels low, as orchids do not survive well if there is a lot of competition from other plants. Remove grass clippings after each mowing.
2 Large plants will establish more quickly and easily than smaller plants.
3 Firm in each plant, and water it well. Do not let the plants dry out in the first year.
4 Introducing good-sized plug plants will mean that they are more likely to flower in the first year after planting.
5 The long-term aim is to produce a mini-meadow that supports a diverse range of plants.

Brassavola perrinii

Widely distributed from Bolivia to north-east Argentina, *B. perrinii*'s long, arching, dark green, grooved, cylindrical leaves, atop skinny pseudobulbs, eventually become pendulous. A showy plant, each inflorescence produces 3–6 starry blooms with triangular, snow-white lips and pale green petals and sepals.

—

Height and spread
25x30cm/10x12in

Temperature
13–24°C/55–75°F

Position
Light summer shade

Flowering time
Spring–summer

WHERE TO GROW

Tolerates a wide range of temperatures, so is a comparatively easy species for an intermediate greenhouse. Apply some shading in summer to prevent greenhouse temperatures becoming too high.

HOW TO GROW

Its pendulous habit makes this species suitable for mounting on a block of tree fern or bark (see Mounting orchids on bark, page 94). Alternatively, grow in a basket in a coarse-grade bark compost (see Growing orchids in a basket, page 84). Use half-strength balanced fertilizer when the roots are active, alternating with rainwater to prevent a build-up of salts.

GROWING TIP

Plants grown on mounts require daily watering either by dipping or spraying; do this in early morning. Allow to dry out between waterings.

MOTH POLLINATION
The flowers are fragrant in the evening and, like other brassavolas, are pollinated by nocturnal moths.

Spider orchid

Brassia verrucosa

This handsome vigorous plant, with large pseudobulbs and dark green foliage, grows in humid tropical forests from Mexico to northern Brazil. Long arching inflorescences bear up to twenty large, strongly scented flowers in two rows. Its long, thin, pale green, spidery petals and sepals are combined with a white lip sporting dark purple warts. A well-grown specimen can flower reliably every year.

Height and spread
20x15cm/8x6in

Temperature
13–24°C/55–75°F

Position
Light shade

Flowering time
Spring–summer

WHERE TO GROW

Grow in an intermediate greenhouse, with some summer shading.

HOW TO GROW

Plant in a medium-grade bark compost in a pot or basket (see Growing orchids in a basket, page 84). Water liberally and feed with a balanced fertilizer during the summer growing period, changing to a high-potash fertilizer such as tomato feed towards autumn.

GROWING TIP

During the spider orchid's winter rest, give only sufficient water to prevent shrivelling of the pseudobulbs.

ORCHID HOTSPOT
Probably the greatest diversity of orchids is to be found in the Andes. The mountainous terrain provides a mosaic of microhabitats that has led to the evolution of a vast array of species. Colombia is home to an amazing 4,270 orchid species.

Bulbophyllum comosum

After its two thin leaves have been shed in autumn, this delightful little orchid from south-east Asia produces a flower spike that resembles a fishing rod. At the end of it is a test-tube brush of dangling, intricate, white flowers, which emit a perfume with a hint of cinnamon.

—

Height and spread
25x30cm/10x12in

Temperature
13–24°C /55–75°F

Position
Light summer shade

Flowering time
Spring

WHERE TO GROW

Grow in the cool or intermediate greenhouse, with some summer shade.

HOW TO GROW

Tie to a piece of cork bark with a pad of sphagnum moss beneath (see Mounting orchids on bark, page 94). Water frequently and fertilize with a half-strength balanced fertilizer throughout summer. As this species is deciduous, reduce watering once the pseudobulbs have ceased increasing in size, and the leaves begin to turn yellow before being shed.

GROWING TIP

Bulbophyllum comosum appreciates an occasional light spraying with rainwater during its winter rest period, to prevent excessive drying of the small pseudobulbs.

THE UNDERGROUND ORCHID

There is an Australian orchid that flowers underground. *Rhizanthella gardneri* is a critically endangered species that grows in Western Australia, and completes its entire life cycle buried in the soil.

Bulbophyllum echinolabium

Height and spread	20x10cm/8x4in
Temperature	13–24°C/55–75°F
Position	Light shade
Flowering time	Spring

Large, dramatic, pale lemon flowers, 35cm/14in long, with red veining, are produced on this vigorous, easy-to-grow plant from Sulawesi. Its mobile lip is the colour of raw meat, and its strong, pungent aroma attracts carrion fly pollinators. Although individual blooms last only three or four days, new flowers appear in succession on the same raceme. *Bulbophyllum echinolabium* flowers on comparatively small pseudobulbs, which develop single, large, broad leaves.

–

WHERE TO GROW

Grow in an intermediate to warm greenhouse, with light shade in summer and high levels of humidity. Reduce watering in winter, without allowing the pseudobulbs to shrivel.

HOW TO GROW

Plant in a pot or basket (see Growing orchids in a basket, page 84) with ample drainage and free-draining compost of equal parts medium-grade bark and sphagnum moss.

GROWING TIP

Beware! Flowers that smell of rotting flesh in general seem to be particularly attractive to slugs and snails, which immediately sniff them out and consume them.

TWO OF A KIND

Boasting more than 1,500 species, *Bulbophyllum* and *Polystachya* are the only pan-tropical genera.

Bulbophyllum lobbii

Growing tropical orchids from a flask of seedlings

As you become more expert at growing orchids, it is worth considering buying flasks of seedlings. Not only is this a less expensive way of acquiring new (and possibly difficult-to-obtain) plants, but it can also be very satisfying to grow orchids from the seedling stage through to flowering. Flasks can be purchased at any time of year, but I would recommend that, as far as possible, you de-flask and transfer the seedlings to compost in spring, as the days are getting longer and temperature and light levels are increasing.

You are much more likely to succeed with ten large, well-grown seedlings than with a flask crammed full of small seedlings. Choose seedlings with well-developed root systems. Ideally, the leaves should almost reach the flask lid (although this does not apply to miniature species). Reject flasks that show signs of contamination with a fungus or bacteria. Likewise, unless the orchid species is deciduous, avoid flasks where leaves are turning yellow or brown.

Plant seedlings into small pots or multi-celled seed trays filled either with sphagnum moss or with a mixture of equal parts fine-grade bark, sphagnum moss and perlite. Some growers prefer to raise their seedlings in so-called 'community pots'; in this case, all ten (or thereabouts) seedlings are placed in a single small pot. It is important to prepare the compost by moistening it at least a day in advance.

The environment within a flask of seedlings will have 100 per cent relative humidity, and it will take some time for the leaves to fully develop a protective waxy cuticle. Therefore, continue to provide such a humid environment by placing the potted seedlings in a propagator, set in a greenhouse or on a suitable windowsill, away from direct sunlight. Once established, give the seedlings half-strength high-nitrogen fertilizer. Pot on seedlings regularly.

1

2

3

4

5

1 Open the flask and remove the seedlings (here *Bulbophyllum echinolabium*) carefully by taking hold of the leaves with a pair of forceps (tweezers).
2 Place the seedlings in a dish of tepid water; wash gently to remove all traces of the agar medium.
3 Fill some small pots or seed trays with pre-moistened sphagnum moss, or a mixture of fine-grade bark and perlite.
4 Insert one or more seedlings in each container, then label with the name of the species (or hybrid) and the date.
5 Cover the seedlings so they have a humid enviroment. Then place in a greenhouse or on a suitable windowsill, away from direct sunlight. A little bottom heat can sometimes help the seedlings to establish, and you may consider using a heated propagator.

Evergreen calanthe

Calanthe striata aka *C. sieboldii*

Height and spread
35x10cm/14x4in

Temperature
–10–24°C/14–75°F

Position
Moderate to light summer shade

Flowering time
Spring

Calanthe consists of two distinct groups, which do not interbreed (and possibly merit separate genera). The evergreen calanthes such as *C. striata* are cool-growing woodland plants from Korea, Japan and China. They form basal rosettes of broad ribbed leaves. Hybrid evergreen calanthes are more vigorous than the species. They produce 25cm/10in spikes of lemon-yellow flowers in spring.

–

WHERE TO GROW

Grow in the garden, or in pots in a cold greenhouse.

HOW TO GROW

In pots use a mixture of two parts loam, one part leafmould and one part perlite. Feed with half-strength balanced fertilizer during the growing season. When planted in the garden, evergreen calanthe requires moist but well-drained soil and, depending on the soil type, may benefit from the addition of organic material.

GROWING TIP

In the garden, protect from excessive winter damp by covering with a cloche.

Tropical calanthe

Calanthe vestita

Found from Assam to New Guinea, this deciduous calanthe possesses characteristically jointed, angular pseudobulbs wrapped in silver papery sheaths. It has slightly hairy racemes, up to 1m/3ft long, bearing long-lasting, white flowers with pink centres.

–

Height and spread
12x4cm/5x1½in

Temperature
13–24°C/55–75°F

Position
Light summer shade

Flowering time
Winter

WHERE TO GROW

Grow in a warm greenhouse with sufficient shade to prevent leaf burn.

HOW TO GROW

When the pseudobulbs begin to shoot in spring, pot in two parts loam, one part leafmould and one part horticultural sand, burying the pseudobulb only sufficiently deep to prevent it from rocking. Resist the temptation to water until the roots are around 10cm/4in long, then water and feed with a balanced fertilizer. When the leaves begin to turn yellow in late summer, give only sufficient water to prevent wilting of the flowers. After leaf fall, keep tropical calanthe cool and dry.

GROWING TIP

Tropical calanthe requires a completely dry rest in winter. Pseudobulbs can be stored on sphagnum moss or dry soil until the new growth appear.

NOTABLE SPECIES AND HYBRIDS

- *C. rosea* has rose-pink blooms that last 1–2 months.
- *C.* x *veitchii* is a vigorous hybrid with a deep pink lip and contrasting white sepals and petals.

FIRST HYBRID

The first man-made orchid hybrid was *Calanthe* Dominii. It was flowered by John Dominy in 1856. The generic name *Calanthe*, derived from the Greek *kalos* (beautiful) and *anthe* (flower), is well-deserved.

Cambria

Height and spread
30x15cm/12x6in

Temperature
13–24°C/55–75°F

Position
Light shade

Flowering time
Winter–spring

The term Cambria is generally applied to a wide variety of related man-made hybrids (see Man-made orchids, page 11). Typically, they are offered for sale with other orchids requiring similar cultural conditions: dancing lady (*Cyrtochilum*), pansy orchids (*Miltoniopsis*), spider orchids (*Brassia*) and *Zygopetalum*. Cambrias have light green foliage and smallish pseudobulbs (7cm/3in tall).

–

WHERE TO GROW

Although they can be raised in an intermediate greenhouse, cambrias are widely sold as windowsill orchids, to be grown in bright but filtered light.

HOW TO GROW

Cambrias often thrive in the steamy atmosphere of a bathroom or kitchen. Be wary of overwatering. Allow the compost to dry out between each watering, but do not allow it to become bone dry. Use a half-strength balanced fertilizer, flushing the compost through with rainwater every third or fourth watering. Reduce watering in winter, once the pseudobulbs are mature. They have thin roots. Cambrias are often sold in peat-based composts. However, when the time comes for repotting, change to a compost that is water-retentive, such as two parts fine- or medium-grade pine bark, one part perlite and one part chopped sphagnum moss. Repot after flowering in spring, as new shoots begin to develop and green tips can be seen developing on the roots.

GROWING TIP

Although cambrias appreciate regular misting in summer, avoid doing so in the middle of the day, as it can cause leaf burn.

AN ORCHID SUPERSTAR
The iconic × *Oncidopsis* (× *Vuylstekeara*) Cambria 'Plush' has been reproduced by tissue culture, and millions sold around the world.

Miltoniopsis phalaenopsis

NOTABLE CULTIVARS

- x *Oncidopsis* (x *Vuylstekeara*) Cambria 'Plush' has striking large flowers, wine-red petals and sepals and beautifully marked, broad white-bordered lips.
- x *Oncidopsis* Nelly Isler produces sprays of large, flat, scarlet blooms.

RIGHT x *Oncidopsis* Nelly Isler is frequently seen for sale in garden centres and orchid nurseries.
BELOW LEFT AND BELOW RIGHT Orchid breeders have produced a startling array of beautifully coloured and patterned Cambrias, which are often sold without names.

Cattleya cernua

aka *Sophronitis cernua*

Bunches of five or six scarlet flowers, each 1cm/½in across, are produced by this charming, desirable, miniature orchid that grows high in the canopy in the Atlantic rainforest of Brazil and northern Argentina. Short racemes push their way through from the apex of each small pseudobulb as the single, dark green leaf opens like two pages of a book.

–

Height and spread
5x12cm/2x5in

Temperature
13–24°C/55–75°F

Position
Sunny

Flowering time
Winter

WHERE TO GROW

The thick, leathery, slightly succulent, grey-green leaves indicate a plant that thrives in sunshine. Grow high in the apex of an intermediate greenhouse.

HOW TO GROW

Cattleya cernua is best grown attached to a piece of cork oak or branch (see Mounting orchids on bark, page 94); it detests being repotted. It produces its roots and shoots in late summer. The plants can then be watered freely until the pseudobulbs have completed their growth.

GROWING TIP

Do not water late in the day as *C. cernua* resents being wet overnight, and may rot.

HUMMINGBIRD POLLINATION

Whereas pollen tends to be yellow, the pollinia of *C. cernua* are indigo. This is thought to act as camouflage, making its hummingbird pollinator less likely to see and wipe the pollinia from its beak.

Cattleya trianae

Although endangered in its tropical dry forest habitat, where it grows in ancient forest giants, Colombia's national flower can also be seen in many town squares and gardens in the Río Magdalena valley. The flowers can last up to five weeks.

–

WHERE TO GROW

In temperate countries *C. trianae* needs a humid atmosphere in an intermediate greenhouse.

HOW TO GROW

A vigorous species; grown well it can produce two growths in one year. Grow in free-draining compost, in a pot with ample drainage, or mount on bark (see Mounting orchids on bark, page 94). Water well and fertilize with a balanced feed throughout the growing season, using just rainwater every fourth watering. *Cattleya trianae* should be given a winter rest.

GROWING TIP

Cattleya roots tend to adhere to the side of the pot and can be damaged when removing the plant for repotting. Only repot when necessary, and when the emerging new roots of the leading pseudobulb are at least 2.5cm/1in long in spring. Unless the plant needs dividing (see Division, page 36), a better solution may be to put the whole pot inside a slightly larger pot, with extra compost gently added to fill the gap .

Height and spread
35x30cm/14–12in

Temperature
13–24°C/55–75°F

Position
Bright light

Flowering time
Winter

A FLORAL LEGACY

An avenue of trees in Guadalupe in the south of Colombia has been planted with large numbers of *C. trianae* by local schoolchildren: a gift to future generations.

Companion planting on a windowsill

Moth orchids (*Phalaenopsis*) are particularly popular windowsill plants, and are available in a wide range of colours, some with stripes or spots, and can remain in flower for many weeks – even months. They are much more tolerant of low temperatures than most sources would suggest and, in centrally heated houses, they can be grown on almost any windowsill. Miltonias, cambrias, miniature cattleyas and paphiopedilums also make suitable subjects for the windowsill. They can all be grown alongside a wide range of suitable (non-orchid) flowering and foliage plants that enjoy the same growing conditions. Not only will these other house plants make an attractive addition to your display, but they will also help to maintain the desired humidity for the orchids.

Select a suitable windowsill: east- or west-facing is good. If the windowsill is in full sun, your plants may require some shading in summer; this can be provided by net curtains, for example. The aim is to gather together plants that enjoy similar light conditions, and to avoid those whose leaves may scorch. If the plant is not happy, try moving it to a different plant grouping on another windowsill. You may need to adapt the positions of your plants during the course of the year: a sunny windowsill that may be ideal in winter may be too hot in summer.

It is vital to create a humid microclimate around your grouped plants. This can be achieved by standing the pots on a tray or container of gravel or, preferably, expanded clay granules, on the windowsill. Keep the moisture-retentive material constantly moist, and the water level slightly below that of the surface of the aggregate. You may find the high relative humidity of a bathroom is ideal.

OTHER COMPANION PLANTS FOR ORCHIDS

Dumb cane (*Dieffenbachia seguine*)
Painted-leaf begonia (*Begonia rex*)
Peace lily (*Spathyphyllum wallisii*)
Peacock plant (*Calathea makoyana*)
Prayer plant (*Maranta leuconeura* var. *kerchoveana*)
Scarlet star (*Guzmania lingulata*)
Spider plant (*Chlorophytum comosum* 'Variegatum')
Tail flower (*Anthurium andraeanum*)
Urn plant (*Aechmea fasciata*)

A Cacti and other succulents (here *Echeveria*, *Rebutia*, *Astrophytum* and *Cereus*) can be grown with your orchid to provide an attractive arrangement.

B Standing your mixture of plants (here a small tank bromeliad, *Masdevallia* Gypsy and variety of *Pilea*) on a tray of moist gravel helps to maintain a humid microclimate

C A wide range of pots can be used to enhance your plants (here *Anthurium*, x *Oncidopsis* Cambria 'Plush'. *Peperomia polybotrya* and daffodils).

Coelia bella

Coelia bella has apple-green, egg-shaped pseudobulbs, with long, narrow, grassy leaves. Short inflorescences of 6–12 tubular, crystalline-white flowers, with rose-purple-tipped sepals and petals and sulphur-yellow lips, appear from the bases of the pseudobulbs in early winter. The flowers last for around a month and give off a delicious perfume reminiscent of bitter almonds or marzipan.

—

Height and spread
35x10cm/14x4in

Temperature
10–24°C/50–75°F

Position
Dappled shade

Flowering time
Winter

WHERE TO GROW

Replicate its natural habitat of humid mountain rainforests in Mexico and Central America by growing *C. bella* on a shady windowsill or in the cool greenhouse.

HOW TO GROW

Grow in a pot with plenty of drainage holes. Its root hairs, which can be seen on emerging roots, indicate that *C. bella* requires a particularly moisture-retentive compost. Grow in a pot in a mixture of two parts sphagnum moss, one part medium-grade bark and one part perlite. Use a balanced fertilizer at half-strength during the growing period, gradually reducing watering in autumn as the pseudobulbs mature.

GROWING TIP

As the roots are particularly sensitive to any build-up of salts, either grow in a specialist terracotta pot with extra slots for drainage, or cut extra drainage holes in a plastic pot.

ORCHIDS AS FOOD
Many terrestrial orchid species are under threat in Zambia and surrounding countries, where they are harvested to make a local delicacy called *chikanda*.

Coelogyne cristata

Height and spread
12x15cm/5x6in

Temperature
10–24°C/50–75°F

Position
Light shade

Flowering time
Spring

Originating from the eastern Himalayas to China, *C. cristata* was once a favourite of local authority parks departments. Enormous greenhouse-grown specimens can sometimes be seen at spring orchid shows, bearing hundreds of large, lightly fragrant, crystalline-white flowers, with egg-yolk-yellow crests, cascading over the sides of the containers.

–

WHERE TO GROW

This easy orchid for the cool greenhouse or windowsill can be grown outdoors in a shady spot in summer.

HOW TO GROW

Grow in a mixture of equal parts medium-grade bark, sphagnum and perlite in a shallow pan, mounted on a tree-fern slab (see Mounting orchids on bark, page 94) or in a basket (see Growing orchids in a basket, page 84). The walnut-sized, spherical or egg-shaped pseudobulbs are widely spaced according to the variety (see below), and allow the rhizomes to scramble over the surface of the compost. Give abundant water during the growing period, followed by a distinct winter rest, when *C. cristata* can be misted from time to time to prevent shrivelling of the pseudobulbs, which resemble fat juicy grapes.

GROWING TIP

Coelogyne cristata resents disturbance and so does not appreciate being repotted.

NOTABLE VARIETIES

- *C. cristata* var. *hololeuca* (aka *C. cristata* var. *alba*) bears completely white flowers and larger, more conical pseudobulbs, which are particularly widely spaced.
- *C. cristata* var. *citrina* (aka *C. cristata* var. *lemoniana*) has lemon-yellow centres to its white flowers.

Cuitlauzina pendula

Height and spread	25x20cm/10x8in
Temperature	10–24°C/50–75°F
Position	Light shade
Flowering time	Spring

In spring, pendent racemes, 75cm/30in long, of up to thirty yellow-crested, white, or pink-flushed white flowers, 5cm/2in across, fill the air of *C. pendula's* Mexican forest home with a delicious lemon scent. The flower spikes emerge along with the new growths. Dark green, flattened pseudobulbs and tough leathery leaves indicate a plant that is subject to seasonal drought.

—

WHERE TO GROW

Grow in a free-draining, bark-based compost in a pot or basket suspended from the greenhouse apex (see Growing orchids in a basket, page 84), or mounted on bark (see Mounting orchids on bark, page 94). Provide light shade throughout summer in a cool greenhouse.

HOW TO GROW

Water and feed with half-strength balanced fertilizer during its summer growing period, gradually withdrawing water in autumn. As long as *C. pendula* is grown in a humid environment, it will tolerate some winter shrivelling of its pseudobulbs.

GROWING TIP

Do not water during its winter rest, but maintain a high relative humidity.

BIT A MYSTERY

The Bornean *Paphiopedilum sanderianum* has helically twisted petals that can grow to 1m/3ft or more in length. Although it has been suggested that such enormously long petals have evolved to aid pollination by a so-far-unidentified pollinator, the truth is that, to date, no one really knows their function.

EPIPHYTE OR LITHOPHYTE, SYMPODIAL

Cymbidium lowianum

Height and spread
45x40cm/18x16in

Temperature
10–24°C/50–75°F

Position
Light shade

Flowering time
Spring–summer

With its large, egg-shaped pseudobulbs and long, strap-like leaves, *C. lowianum* produces spikes of thirty or more large, yellow-green, well-spaced flowers, with a distinctive, reddish brown V-shape on the apex of each lip.

—

WHERE TO GROW

Grow in a cool greenhouse or conservatory. Plants can be cultivated outdoors in a shady spot in summer and brought inside before the first frosts.

HOW TO GROW

Plant in a free-draining compost such as coarse-grade pine bark. Maintain a buoyant, moist atmosphere in the greenhouse year-round; if the atmosphere is too dry, *C. lowianum* is vulnerable to red spider mite (see Pests, page 134). Water well in the growing season. Plants require good light, with only sufficient shade to prevent scorching of the leaves, and a distinct winter rest. This heavy feeder needs half-strength, high-potash fertilizer (tomato feed) throughout the growing season to induce flowering, using rainwater every fourth watering. To display the flower spikes to their best advantage see Training flower spikes, page 102.

FLUSHED WITH SUCCESS
The lips of cymbidium flowers blush pink after being successfully pollinated.

GROWING TIP

A common complaint is that cymbidiums are difficult to flower. Often this is because the plants have been grown indoors in a consistently warm environment, where they produce beautiful, dark green foliage – but no flowers. The key to stimulating flowering is often to give plants a cool period outdoors in autumn.

Repotting a cymbidium

As long as the compost is not breaking down, some orchids can be allowed to grow for a number of years without repotting. Cattleyas and cymbidiums, for example, have a tendency to sulk when repotted – refusing to flower the following season. Growers often wait to repot these two genera until the lead growths have escaped the confines of the pot, and the roots are either happily growing in mid-air or, particularly if it is terracotta, clinging tenaciously to the side of the pot. However, cymbidiums, cattleyas and the cattleya relatives do benefit from regular repotting. This should be done before the compost begins to break down and, in the case of plants with pseudobulbs, once the leading growth has reached the edge of the pot.

Plants are normally repotted in spring, when the roots become active. If the plant is very large, it can be divided into a number of pieces (see Division, page 36). Each division should consist of a minimum of three backbulbs (i.e. pseudobulbs that have lost their leaves) and three growths with leaves.

After repotting, take care not to overwater. The plant may benefit from a daily spray with rainwater.

1. Soak the fresh potting compost overnight before using.
2. Remove the plant (here a cymbidium hybrid) by inverting the pot over a tray to catch the compost. Gently wash off the old compost and discard. Try to minimize damage to the roots.
3. Trim any dead roots with clean scissors, sharp knife or secateurs. Healthy roots are plump and creamy white. Dead roots are brown and flat, with the outer layer (the velamen) easily separating from a stringy core.
4. Carefully peel back and remove any dead leaf bracts.
5. Leaving a minimum of three pseudobulbs, use a sterilized knife to sever carefully the rhizome and separate the old pseudobulbs.
6. Half fill a suitable-sized, clean pot. Set the newly divided plant in it, against the side of the rim, with the growing point facing the middle of the pot. Allow sufficient space for a further two years of growth. Spread out the roots.
7. Add more the compost, gently easing it between the roots with your fingers. Firm the compost slightly, then topdress. Label the plant. If the root system is poor, you may need to stake the plant with a cane.

1

2

3

4

5

6

7

Showy orchid

Cypripedium reginae

This is a temperate slipper orchid. With its striking pink lip contrasting with white sepals and petals, and pale green, downy foliage, it is the loveliest of North American lady slipper orchids and deserves its common name as showy orchid. With flower spikes up to 90cm/36in long, it is one of the tallest slipper orchids and can soon form a large clump. Unusually for a slipper orchid, rather than being a typically woodland species, showy orchid thrives in boggy conditions. A lovely, white-flowered form is also available.

–

Height and spread
60x20cm/24x8in

Temperature
–10–24°C/14–75°F

Position
Full sun to dappled shade

Flowering time
Summer

WHERE TO GROW

Plant in a pot in a moisture-retentive but free-draining compost of two parts loam, one part leafmould and one part perlite, in a cold frame or cold greenhouse. In temperate regions, grow in suitable garden soil, in specially prepared beds or in pots sunk into the ground, in dappled shade.

HOW TO GROW

In the greenhouse, showy orchid requires some shade in summer. Protect in winter from excess moisture, particularly when temperatures are below freezing. Repot when dormant (see Repotting a cypripedium, page 68).

GROWING TIP

Showy orchid tolerates more water than other cypripediums, and it should never be allowed to dry out.

ACCESSIBLE FOR ALL
Over recent years, breeders have produced many easily grown, garden-worthy *Cypripedium* hybrids in a wide range of colours, which are now available at reasonable prices in orchid nurseries and garden centres.

Dancing lady

Cyrtochilum flexuosum aka *Oncidium flexuosum*, golden rain

Long branched spikes carry an abundance of golden flowers on this South American orchid. Each individual bloom has a broad, yellow, skirt-like lip, while its petals and sepals are sprinkled with red-brown freckles. Dancing lady has large flattened pseudobulbs, strap-shaped, floppy leaves and thin roots.

Height and spread
35x30cm/14x12in

Temperature
10–24°C/50–75°F

Position
Light shade

Flowering time
Autumn

–

WHERE TO GROW

Grow in a cool greenhouse or on a windowsill. Dancing lady requires light shade in the middle of the day in summer, to prevent leaf burn.

HOW TO GROW

Grow in a free-draining mixture of two parts fine-grade pine bark, one part perlite and one part sphagnum moss. Maintain a moist atmosphere year-round. Water well and feed with half-strength balanced fertilizer throughout the growing season, allowing the compost to dry out between waterings. Give a winter rest, with just sufficient water to prevent the compost drying out completely. Overwatering in winter can cause the pseudobulbs to rot.

SMALLEST ORCHID
The miniscule *Platystele jungermannioides* has flowers that are a mere 2.1mm/1/12in wide and petals that are only one cell thick.

GROWING TIP

Repot when the new growths begin to emerge and roots can grow into fresh compost. In well-grown plants, the pseudobulbs will become progressively larger year on year and may need repotting after two years of growth.

Repotting a cypripedium

Repot during the plant's dormant period, usually in autumn or spring, before it commences new growth. As with most other orchids, the key to success lies in growing cypripedium in a free-draining compost. A number of recipes are available, but a mixture of two parts loam, one part leafmould and one part either perlite or horticultural gravel is usually satisfactory.

Although often subject to below-freezing temperatures in their natural habitats, cypripediums are often protected in winter by a blanket of snow, and their rhizomes are not subject to a potentially lethal combination of cold and wet. Therefore, after repotting in autumn, place the pots in a cold frame or cold greenhouse, where they can be sunk into a bed of sand. Good air circulation is essential. After repotting in spring, sink the pot into the ground in the garden (see Showy orchid, page 66).

1 Remove the plant (here a cypripedium hybrid) from its pot, taking care not to damage the slightly brittle roots. Remove any dead leaves and gently wash off any remaining soil.
2 Select a suitable-sized, clean pot that will allow for several years of growth. Place drainage material such as large-grade pumice in the bottom of the pot. Make a mound of compost in the middle of the pot. Place the plant on top of the mound, so that the shoots are in the centre, and carefully arrange the roots so that they radiate towards the edge of the pot.
3 Cover the roots with compost, leaving the shoots exposed.
4 Topdress with drainage material such as coarse gravel, but allow sufficient space for water. Replace the label.
5 Plants can be brought indoors and kept on a cool windowsill while you enjoy the flowers, such as this white form of the showy orchid (*Cypripedium reginae*).

1

2

3

4

5

Cyrtochilum macranthum

Height and spread
45x30cm/18x12in

Temperature
10–24°C/50–75°F

Position
Bright light

Flowering time
Autumn

A well-flowered plant of *C. macranthum* is a spectacular sight with its amazingly long, branched racemes, to 4m/13ft long, carrying numerous large, wavy-margined, mustard-yellow flowers, 9cm/3½in across, each with a contrasting, triangular, purple-tinged lip. This large plant has somewhat pear-shaped pseudobulbs and long leaves.

—

WHERE TO GROW

Because it originates in misty cloud forests from Colombia to northern Peru, *C. macranthum* should be grown in a cool humid greenhouse.

HOW TO GROW

Grow in a pot in medium-grade bark compost, or mounted on bark (see Mounting orchids on bark, page 94)

GROWING TIP

In its natural habitat the vine-like inflorescence scrambles over the vegetation, and can be found hanging from trees along riversides. As soon as a flower spike develops, begin training it over a frame, or along a wire in the greenhouse (see Training flower spikes, page 102).

WORLD'S LARGEST ORCHID

South-east Asia's tiger orchid (*Grammatophyllum speciosum*) is reputedly the world's largest orchid. The immense leafy stems can each reach several metres in length. It created a sensation in 2015, when it flowered at the Royal Botanic Gardens, Kew.

Common spotted orchid

Dactylorhiza fuchsii

Height and spread
30x15cm/12x6in

Temperature
–10–24°C/14–75°F

Position
Full sun to moderate shade

Flowering time
Summer

Rosettes of often beautifully patterned, dark green leaves emerge in late spring, producing tall spikes of white or pinkish white flowers with scribbled markings on the lips. Occurring throughout Europe and Asia, common spotted orchids can be found blooming in their thousands in meadows and around woodland margins. The closely related southern marsh orchid (*D. praetermissa*) is another desirable garden plant, but requires wetter conditions such as a pond margin.

—

WHERE TO GROW

Plant in a sunny or slightly shady spot, or else grow in pots in a cold greenhouse with moderate shade.

HOW TO GROW

Common spotted orchids are summergreen, meaning that their above-ground parts die down over winter. Grow in a free-draining, soil-based compost. Do not allow the compost or garden soil to dry out in summer. When grown in pots or containers in the garden, seedlings sometimes appear in other pots or containers, as if by magic. Common spotted orchids can be propagated from seed using the method outlined in Growing a dactylorhiza from seed (see page 72).

GROWING TIP

If growing common spotted orchid in a pot, place a piece of fine mesh or shade cloth over the drainage holes to prevent the entry of slugs and snails.

ALL IN A NAME
The underground tubers of common spotted orchid resemble little hands. The name *Dactylorhiza* literally means finger roots (*dactylos* = finger, *rhiza* = root).

Growing a dactylorhiza from seed

Although the idea of growing orchids from seed may appear a little daunting or, without a sophisticated laboratory, to be beyond the capabilities of the average gardener, it is possible to do so using little more than the equipment available in the average kitchen. For example, common spotted orchid (*Dactylorhiza fuchsii*; see page 71) is easily grown on a simple medium made up of finely ground porridge oats and agar that is inoculated with a compatible symbiotic fungus (available from orchid societies). The fungus will fan out across the medium.

To make 1 litre/1¾ pints of the oats medium, weigh 3.5g/⅛oz oats and 6g/⅕oz agar, and transfer to a large jug. Add a little cold water, and mix to a smooth paste. Gradually pour in 1 litre/1¾ pints boiling water and stir until the oats and agar have dissolved. Blitz in a liquidizer or food processor, or rub through a sieve to a smooth consistency. Sterilize the medium by heating in a screw-top jar in a pressure cooker or in a microwave for twenty minutes. Take care to ensure that the lid is loose. Allow the medium to cool until the jar can be held comfortably in the hand. Pour into sterile jars or Petri dishes until needed. Then sterilize the seed before adding the oats medium and innoculated agar to trigger germination. Once large enough, transplant the seedling into a mix of equal parts soil-based compost and grit or perlite, either in spring or in autumn.

1. Make a 2.5cm/1in square envelope using unbleached coffee filter paper.
2. Add a small amount of seed, and staple closed.
3. To sterilize the seed, drop the envelope in a jar of 10 per cent household bleach. Agitate gently for about ten minutes.
4. Wash the envelope in sterile (boiled) water for two minutes.
5. To transfer the seed to the surface of the agar jelly, remove the envelope from the jar of water, and open it with sterile scissors. Then dab the opened envelope on the surface of the jelly medium. The seed will stick to the jelly.
6. Add a small cube of agar containing the fungus. Keep the jar in the dark at room temperature.

1

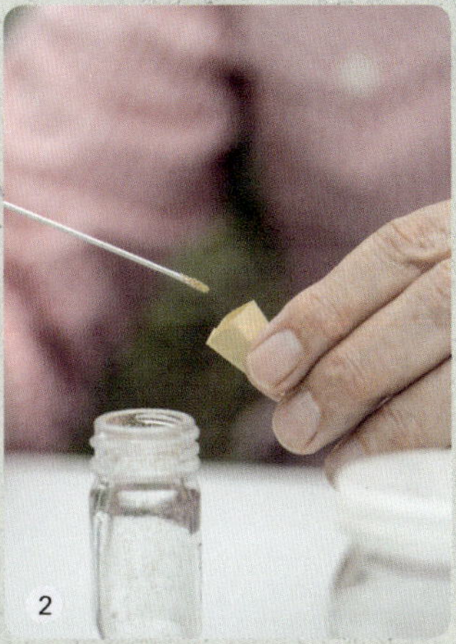
2

3

4

5

6

Dendrobium bigibbum

Height and spread
20x10cm/8x4in
Temperature
13–24°C/55–75°F
Position
Light summer shade
Flowering time
Spring–summer

Tall, cylindrical, slightly club-shaped pseudobulbs with alternate, glossy, dark green leaves produce arching flowering stems bearing up to twenty lilac-purple blooms from their apices. Cooktown orchid (*D. bigibbum* var. *phalaenopsis*) is the floral emblem of Queensland, where it grows on trees and rocks in rainforests, coastal scrub, near rivers, in swamps and open forests.

—

WHERE TO GROW

As it is planted outdoors in its tropical home, *D. bigibbum* should be grown in an intermediate to warm humid greenhouse in temperate regions. It appreciates lots of light, but some shading may be necessary to prevent leaf burn in summer.

HOW TO GROW

Grow mounted (see Mounting orchids on bark, page 94) or in a well-drained pot in a sunny position. Reduce watering in autumn, and keep dry in winter, without allowing the compost to become bone dry. Refrain from watering the new growths as they emerge in spring, until they are at least 5cm/2in tall.

GROWING TIP

Avoid sudden drops in temperature when *D. bigibbum* is in bud, as this can lead to bud drop.

STICKY STUFF

In pre-Columbian Mexico, mucilage was extracted from the pseudobulbs of various orchids to make a paste that was used to glue feathers on to ceremonial garments.

Dendrobium cuthbertsonii

Height and spread
2.5x7cm/1x3in

Temperature
10–24°C/50–75°F

Position
Dappled summer shade

Flowering time
Spring

This diminutive species from the orchid wonderland that is New Guinea is much coveted by orchid growers. It has compact tufts of dark green, slightly warty leaves and long-lasting, glistening, jewel-like flowers. Originally in scarlets and crimson, *D. cuthbertsonii* is now available in a rainbow of colours from purple, through pinks to yellows and whites, and the occasional bicolour.

WHERE TO GROW

Grow in a cool greenhouse or a terrarium (see Planting up a terrarium, page 116), to reflect its native habitat of moss and cloud forests in mountains above 2,000m (6,560ft) above sea level, where it is subject to almost daily rainfall, and a sharp drop in temperature at night.

HOW TO GROW

Often considered a challenge, *D. cuthbertsonii* can be grown successfully in small pots in sphagnum moss. It resents hot dry conditions for any length of time, and the moss should be kept constantly moist. Feed weekly with quarter- or half-strength balanced fertilizer, flushing the compost through with rainwater every three weeks. Apply light shade in summer.

GROWING TIP

Keep constantly moist and never allow to dry out. This orchid benefits from twice daily misting with rainwater: once in the early morning, and then later in the evening.

AMONG THE LARGEST
With more than 1,400 species, and along with *Bulbophyllum, Dendrobium* is one of the largest genera in the orchid family. Many of these brightly coloured orchid gems grow in the highlands of New Guinea.

Dendrobium kingianum

Height and spread
25x20cm/10x8in

Temperature
5–24°C/41–75°F

Position
Moderate to bright light

Flowering time
Winter

Common in eastern Australia, this variable species can produce either clumps of short and stout pseudobulbs, or long and thin ones, depending on the plant's origin. Each pseudobulb bears 2–4 leaves towards its tip. A single raceme appears from the apex of each mature pseudobulb, with as many as fifteen flowers. When in bloom, a well-grown *D. kingianum* is a haze of tiny, lilac-pink flowers, each with a contrasting dark lip.

—

WHERE TO GROW
Grow in a cool greenhouse with some summer shade, or on a bright windowsill.

HOW TO GROW
Plant in a pot using a free-draining bark compost. Water copiously and feed during summer months, reducing water during its winter rest. Although *D. kingianum* appears to enjoy being slightly pot-bound, it should be repotted annually. It has a strong tendency to produce keikis, which can be removed and potted on to produce additional plants (see Keikis, page 36).

GROWING TIP
Dendrobium kingianum normally requires a cold stimulus during its winter rest period to induce flowering, so transfer to a cooler location for its rest.

AN OVERNIGHT STAY
After searching for somewhere to stay overnight, solitary bees sometimes hunker down inside the flowers of Mediterranean tongue orchids (*Serapias*).

Noble orchid

Dendrobium nobile

When in bloom, the tall, plump, stem-like pseudobulbs of noble orchid are often referred to as canes, and are covered from top to bottom with large flowers, 6–8cm/2½–3¼in across, typically pale mauve, with a striking, deep purple eye. The hybrids of this Asian species are frequently for sale in garden centres.

Height and spread
25x10cm/10x4in

Temperature
13–24°C/55–75°F

Position
Light summer shade

Flowering time
Spring

—

WHERE TO GROW

Grow in an intermediate or warm greenhouse or on a windowsill, with plenty of light and humidity.

HOW TO GROW

Get the plants growing as soon as possible in a medium-grade bark compost in spring, and keep them growing until the final terminal leaf is formed at the apex of each cane. Water and fertilize frequently in summer, gradually reducing water towards autumn. After losing its leaves in autumn, give noble orchid a cool, frost-free, dry rest in winter, to induce flowering.

GROWING TIP

Flower buds begin to appear on the nodes of the canes in early spring, at which time, if given the slightest whiff of water, the buds will develop as keikis instead of flowers (see Keikis, page 36). Refrain from watering until you are certain that you can see distinct flower buds. This species can be propagated by stem cuttings (see Cuttings, page 37).

LONG LIFE AND HAPPINESS

When ground, the canes of *D. nobile* are said to be an aphrodisiac and to impart longevity. As a result, this species is at risk of extinction in the wild because of over-collection for traditional Chinese medicine.

Dendrobium speciosum

Height and spread
30x15cm/12x6in

Temperature
13–24°C/55–75°F

Position
Bright light

Flowering time
Winter–spring

Native to eastern Australia is *D. speciosum*, a truly spectacular plant when in bloom. Each stem-like pseudobulb, or cane, bears a number of inflorescences, each to 60cm/24in long, with up to one hundred waxy, slightly spidery, long-lasting, white to creamy yellow, scented flowers.

–

WHERE TO GROW

This robust, drought-tolerant garden plant in its native Australia requires bright light with good air movement when grown in an intermediate greenhouse in temperate regions.

HOW TO GROW

Preferably, attach to a tree fern or cork-oak mount (see Mounting orchids on bark, page 94). Because it is such a vigorous grower, if container grown *D. speciosum* needs frequent repotting. Feed with half-strength high-nitrogen fertilizer from spring to early summer, changing to a high-potash one such as tomato feed in autumn. Water with rainwater every third watering. Allow the compost to dry out between waterings. Reduce watering in autumn, but do not allow plants to dry out completely. Increase watering (and begin feeding) when new growths begin to develop in spring.

GROWING TIP

Give a distinct winter rest without watering, to induce flowering.

ENERGY FROM ITS ROOTS

Ghost orchid (*Dendrophylax lindenii*) grows in the swamps of the Florida Everglades and western Cuba, and is one of the so-called leafless orchids, with photosynthesis confined to its roots.

Pride of Table Mountain

Disa uniflora

Height and spread
10x20cm/4x8in

Temperature
5–24°C/41–75°F

Position
Light shade

Flowering time
Spring–summer

Despite its scientific name, a flower spike of pride of Table Mountain often bears two or more large, triangular, vibrant red blooms, which last for a number of weeks. After flowering, the plant gradually dies down. New shoots emerge from an underground tuber towards autumn.

–

WHERE TO GROW

Grow in a frost-free greenhouse with some light shade, or on a shady windowsill. Plants can be placed in a shady location outdoors during summer.

HOW TO GROW

Grow in a mixture of equal parts sphagnum moss and perlite. Pride of Table Mountain likes to have its feet in cold water, so stand the pot in a tray of rainwater and also water frequently from the top with fresh cold rainwater. Repot into fresh compost annually in autumn. This orchid often produces more than one tuber, and these can be potted up separately. It can be propagated by sowing seed on sphagnum moss (see Sowing disas, page 35).

GROWING TIP

It is essential that only rainwater is used, as pride of Table Mountain is intolerant of any salt build-up. In nature this orchid grows on the banks of cool mountain streams. Plants grown in tap water rapidly decline and die.

WOW FACTOR
Disa hybrids can be found in a wide palette of electrifying, even fluorescent, colours at the yellow, orange and red end of the spectrum.

Vampire orchid

Dracula chimaera

Height and spread
15x10cm/6x4in

Temperature
10–24°C/50–75°F

Position
Dappled shade

Flowering time
Spring

Who can resist growing such an exotically named orchid? The strange, other-worldly flowers, which hang suspended like triangular flying saucers by a thread from the parent plant, must be viewed from below to appreciate the pale inflated lips that resemble the undersides of mushrooms or toadstools. They are surrounded by cinnamon-spotted, broad, cream, long-tailed sepals, which are covered with hairs. Vampire orchid flowers are pollinated by fungus gnats.

—

WHERE TO GROW

Grow in a shaded cool greenhouse to replicate their native habitat of moss-covered trees in cloud forests.

HOW TO GROW

Plant in a mixture of equal parts sphagnum moss and perlite, and mount (see Mounting orchids on bark, page 94) or grow in a basket (see Growing orchids in a basket, page 84) because the inflorescences are pendent and emerge from the bottom of the vampire orchid.

GROWING TIP

Keep vampire orchid constantly moist and never let it dry out. Mist frequently with rainwater.

LITTLE CREATURES
The generic name *Dracula* means little dragon. Vampire orchid is just one of around ninety species that are found in moist forests from southern Mexico to Peru. They often have strange monkey faces.

TERRESTRIAL, SYMPODIAL

Chatterbox orchid

Epipactis gigantea

The apical lobe of each lip moves up and down in the breeze so it is known in North America as chatterbox orchid. Up to fifteen well-spaced flowers appear on slender stems, 50cm/20in long, clothed in widely spaced, bright green, downy, pleated leaves. Each small flower is an essay in subtle oranges and browns, and rewards closer examination.

Height and spread
50x15cm/20x6in

Temperature
–10–24°C/14–75°F

Position
Sun or partial shade

Flowering time
Summer

—

WHERE TO GROW

Grow in a cold greenhouse in a pot or shallow pan. Otherwise, as chatterbox orchid grows naturally by the sides of streams and marshy places, plant it in the garden in pond margins or in a bog garden.

HOW TO GROW

Plant the slender rhizome in a mixture of equal parts loam, leafmould and either horticultural sand or perlite.

GROWING TIP

Cover outdoor plants with a mulch over winter, to prevent it from freezing.

FLORAL RECORD-BREAKER
With a total of 1,684 flowers, a chatterbox orchid holds the Guinness World Record for the most blooms on a sympodial orchid.

Guaria morada

Guarianthe skinneri

Height and spread	35x30cm/14x12in
Temperature	13–24°C/55–75°F
Position	Light shade
Flowering time	Winter–spring

Costa Rica's national flower is *Guaria morada*, huge specimen plants of which grown in baskets can be seen at their national and international orchid shows. In its natural habitat, club-shaped pseudobulbs are typically topped by dense heads of pale purple flowers. Breeders have, however, selected a wide range of colour varieties, from snow-white to rich purples with dark centres. *Guaria morada*'s attractiveness has probably been its undoing. Both over-collection and loss of habitat have led to its almost complete disappearance from the wild in Costa Rica.

—

WHERE TO GROW

Although it can be cultivated outside in warm regions such as Florida, *Guaria morada* is suitable for an intermediate greenhouse or a windowsill in more temperate climates.

HOW TO GROW

Grow in a pot in a medium-grade bark compost, or mount on bark (see Mounting orchids on bark, page 94). Water well and fertilize with a balanced feed in the growing season, using just rainwater every fourth watering. Give *Guaria morada* a winter rest.

GROWING TIP

Guaria morada appreciates plenty of light throughout the year, with some summer shading.

ANTS IN YOUR PLANTS
Myrmecophila tibicinis actively encourages ants as a defence against herbivores by having hollow pseudobulbs in which the ants nest.

Habenaria medusa

Height and spread
7x12cm/3x5in

Temperature
13–24°C/55–75°F

Position
Summer shade

Flowering time
Autumn

Extraordinary flowers emerge from the centre of a rosette of bright green leaves on this deciduous orchid from the monsoon grasslands of Indonesia. Each bloom is a white starburst on a spike growing up to 50cm/20in long, with as many as twenty flowers creating a firework display. A long nectary combined with a sweet evening fragrance suggest a flower that is moth-pollinated.

—

WHERE TO GROW

Grow on a sunny windowsill with some light summer shade.

HOW TO GROW

Gradually reduce watering when the leaves begin to die down after flowering in autumn, ahead of giving the plant its winter rest. Store the tuber somewhere cool and dry, without allowing it to shrivel. The following spring, repot in a terracotta pot in a moisture-retentive but free-draining compost of equal parts medium-grade bark and sphagnum moss. Resist the temptation to water until the new shoot emerges.

GROWING TIP

When buying *H. medusa*, select the largest fattest tuber if you want it to flower soon. A well-grown plant will produce multiple new tubers over time.

TREASURE TROVE
With around 400,000 preserved specimens, the Royal Botanic Gardens, Kew has the world's largest and most comprehensive orchid herbarium.

PROJECT 7

Growing orchids in a basket

Epiphytic orchids often grow better in a basket or when mounted than in a pot (see also Mounting orchids on bark, page 94). Indeed, it is not practical to grow some species in pots because of the pendulous habit of their flower spikes. If epiphytic orchids were grown in conventional plant pots, the flower spikes would not be able to escape and would rot in the compost.

Plants can look particularly attractive if grown in specially made teak baskets. Plastic-covered wire baskets or aquarium pots also make suitable containers, or you can create your own from chicken wire. Line the basket with sphagnum moss or coconut fibre and fill with the appropriate compost (see individual plant profiles, pages 38–129).

Suspend baskets high up, in a position where they receive appropriate light as well as free drainage and good air movement. In Thailand, vandas and dendrobiums are grown under shade cloth in baskets with no compost at all.

1 Select a suitable-sized basket – one that will allow for two or three years of new growth – and line it with sphagnum moss or coconut fibre.
2 Place the rear of the orchid (here *Laelia anceps*) against one side of the basket and spread out the roots in a fan.
3 Add the compost, gently teasing it between the roots and making sure that the plant is firmly in place, without any rocking. Water in.
4 Hang in a position that has the appropriate light levels for the plant.

Laelia anceps

Height and spread
20x25cm/8x10in

Temperature
10–24°C (50–75°F)

Position
Bright light

Flowering time
Winter

This robust plant has rhomboid pseudobulbs, each carrying a single, dark green, leathery leaf. Some 3–5, pale lavender flowers, with a delicate honey scent, are borne on a spike 60–90cm/2–3ft long. There are many beautiful clones, and you can have different clones of *L. anceps* in bloom for two or three months from mid-winter onwards.

–

WHERE TO GROW

Plant in a cool greenhouse. Although *L. anceps* can be grown in a pot with ample drainage, its scrambling habit often makes it easier to manage in a basket (see Growing orchids in a basket, page 84) or when mounted on a piece of cork-oak bark (see Mounting orchids on bark, page 94).

HOW TO GROW

Laelia anceps thrives in high light levels; shade only to prevent scorching. Grow in free-draining compost. Water well and fertilize with a balanced feed throughout the growing season. Flush through with rainwater every fourth watering. Give a distinct winter rest, without allowing the pseudobulbs to shrivel. The roots can be sprayed occasionally with rainwater at this time.

GROWING TIP

Flower spikes sometimes dry off and the flower buds fail to develop. This is usually due to a dry atmosphere. Remedy this by regularly damping down the greenhouse floor.

MEXICAN CULTURE
The many beautiful laelias are much loved by Mexicans and occupy a special place in their culture. Illegally collected *L. speciosa* is still seen for sale on Mexican market stalls, when it flowers in May.

Lepanthes calodictyon

Height and spread	20x5cm/8x2in
Temperature	10–24°C/50–75°F
Position	Shade
Flowering time	Year-round

Lepanthes are the miniature jewels of the Central and South American cloud forests. *Lepanthes calodictyon* is especially suitable for growing in a terrarium. It is cultivated primarily for its attractive, crinkled-margined, light green leaves, overlaid by dark green tessellations.

—

WHERE TO GROW

Grow in a humid cool greenhouse or a terrarium (see Planting up a terrarium, page 116).

HOW TO GROW

Mount *L. calodictylon* on a pad of sphagnum moss on a small piece of cork oak or tree fern (see Mounting orchids on bark, page 94), to which the fine roots will adhere.

GROWING TIP

Spray early in the morning with rainwater, and again in the late evening if the weather has been hot. Never allow plants to dry out for more than short periods.

ORIENTAL FAVOURITES
Japanese growers are particularly fond of the smaller-growing species such as *Cymbidium goeringii*, which are appreciated for their variegated leaves, and are grown in special pots.

Leptotes bicolor

Height and spread
10x10cm/4x4in

Temperature
13–24°C/55–75°F

Position
Bright light

Flowering time
Spring–summer

Leptotes bicolor is a small plant occurring from Brazil to Paraguay, with characteristic short, fat, cylindrical leaves that soon form a compact clump. The leaves become mottled with maroon spots in bright light. Pretty pendent flowers, 5cm/2in across, with ivory sepals and petals and a contrasting violet blotch on each slightly pinched lip, last around three weeks. A well-grown specimen covered in blooms makes a lovely sight.

–

WHERE TO GROW
Enjoys bright light, but generally benefits from some summer shade. Grow in an intermediate greenhouse or on a windowsill.

HOW TO GROW
Although *L. bicolor* can be grown in a small pot, because of the pendulous habit of its flowers it is better mounted on a piece of cork oak or tree fern (see Mounting orchids on bark, page 94), to which the roots will soon adhere. The roots may be active throughout the year, but watering (without fertilizing) should be reduced in winter.

GROWING TIP
Allow to dry out between waterings. If grown on a mount *L. bicolor* benefits from an occasional dip in a water bath.

ORCHID FLAVOURING
The flowers and seed capsules of *L. bicolor* contain vanillin and are sometimes used in Brazil as a vanilla substitute.

Jewel orchid

Ludisia discolor

A rainforest species from south-east Asia, jewel orchid is grown primarily for its beautiful, golden-veined, dark green leaves, with a pinkish reverse, that can be enjoyed year-round. It produces 15cm/6in spikes of pretty, curiously twisted, white flowers with lemon-yellow centres.

—

Height and spread
12x15cm/5x6in

Temperature
13–24°C/55–75°F

Position
Dappled shade

Flowering time
Autumn–winter

WHERE TO GROW

Grow in a shady spot in a shallow pan on a windowsill, an intermediate greenhouse or a terrarium (see Planting up a terrarium, page 116).

HOW TO GROW

Grow in a mixture of equal parts medium-grade bark, sphagnum moss and perlite. Keep the compost moist, but be aware that jewel orchid's thick succulent rhizomes are prone to rot if they remain wet for long periods. Remove any remaining water from leaves with a tissue after watering. The plant has a scrambling habit and benefits from annual repotting.

GROWING TIP

Jewel orchids can be propagated easily from long stem cuttings (see Cuttings, page 37). When placed in a jar of water, they will produce roots in a few weeks.

AN ORCHID JIGSAW PUZZLE
The Andes provide a mosaic of microhabitats, which means that many *Lepanthes* species have very restricted distributions. As a result, many species are endangered because of habitat loss.

Lycaste aromatica

Height and spread
30x20cm/12x8in

Temperature
13–24°C/55–75°F

Position
Summer shade

Flowering time
Spring–summer

Clusters of bright orange-yellow flowers, with a spicy cinnamon fragrance, emerge from the bases of the pseudobulbs as the new shoots begin to appear in spring. Ribbed plicate leaves crown pseudobulbs armed with sharp spines on their apices. In Central America *L. aromatica* grows as an epiphyte in cool mixed-oak forests, or lithophytically in mats of thick humus.

—

WHERE TO GROW

Grow this compact orchid in a pot or half-pan in an intermediate greenhouse or on a windowsill. Provide light shade in summer to prevent the leaves from scorching.

HOW TO GROW

Use a free-draining compost mix of equal parts fine-grade orchid bark, perlite and sphagnum moss. Fertilize and water copiously throughout the growing season, maintaining a moist atmosphere. Give a distinct winter rest after the leaves have been shed in autumn, without allowing the pseudobulbs to shrivel.

GROWING TIP

Repot when new growth begins to emerge so the roots can grow into fresh compost. The thin leaves of *L. aromatica* are prone to red spider mite infestations (seee Pests, page 134).

SEX CHANGE
Not all orchids are hermaphrodites: *Catasetum*, for example, has male and female flowers on separate plants.

Masdevallia hybrids

Height and spread
15x15cm/6x6in

Temperature
10–24°C/50–75°F

Position
Dappled shade

Flowering time
Spring–summer

Extensive breeding has produced masdevallias with increased hybrid vigour, making them easier to grow than many of the species (see *Masdevallia rosea*, page 92). They are available in a kaleidoscope of vibrant, often luminous reds, yellows and oranges, some with stripes or spots. A well-grown plant can produce an abundance of spectacular, triangular, arrowhead flowers.

–

WHERE TO GROW

Grow in a shaded cool greenhouse, in a terrarium (see Planting up a terrarium, page 116) or on a windowsill out of direct sunlight on a tray of moist gravel, to create a humid microclimate.

HOW TO GROW

Plant in a mixture of equal parts fine-grade bark, perlite and sphagnum moss. Because masdevallias have fleshy leaves (rather than pseudobulbs) and thin roots, they need a consistently moist (not wet) compost.

GROWING TIP

Additional humidity can be achieved by growing masdevallias in the company of suitable companion plants such as ferns (see Companion planting on a windowsill, page 58).

HIGH-ALTITUDE TRANSFORMATION

Not all orchids are beautiful. *Aa hartwegii* growing at 4,100m/13,500ft above sea level in the páramos of Ecuador and Venezuela looks more like a piece of dead grass than an orchid.

Masdevallia Gypsy

SOME NOTABLE HYBRIDS

- *M.* Copper Angel, with vibrant orange flowers, is a heat-tolerant hybrid that makes a good beginner's masdevallia.
- *M.* Charisma is a cool-grower, with deep purple stripes on a lighter background.
- *M.* Gypsy is taller, to 20cm/8in, with deep red flowers.

Masdevallia rosea

Height and spread
15x15cm/6x6in

Temperature
10–24°C/50–75°F

Position
Dappled shade

Flowering time
Spring–summer

Most of the more than 300 species belonging to this genus from Central and South America are cloud-forest epiphytes, while a small number grow in slightly warmer habitats. One of the prettiest of the genus, *M. rosea*, is a cool-growing, compact plant with tufts of spoon-shaped, dark green leaves and triangular flowers resembling rose-pink arrowheads with tails. What appear to be petals are actually sepals. *Masdevallia rosea* is pollinated by hummingbirds.

–

WHERE TO GROW

Grow in dappled shade only in a humid cool greenhouse, with good air movement; a windowsill is not suitable for this species.

HOW TO GROW

Plant in a pot in a compost of equal parts fine-grade pine bark, perlite and sphagnum; keep the compost constantly moist, but not wet.

GROWING TIP

If positioned on a windowsill, maintain a high relative humidity by standing *M. rosea* on a tray of moist gravel or expanded clay granules, for example.

MACHU PICCHU
The Historic Sanctuary of Machu Picchu, high in the Peruvian Andes, is home to more than 300 species of orchid, including many masdevallias.

OTHER NOTABLE SPECIES

- *M. coccinea* typically has deep rose flowers, but is available in a range of colours. It reaches 30cm/12in tall and must be grown cool.
- *M. tovarensis* has snow-white flowers, is 15cm/6in tall and is relatively easy to grow.

Maxillaria tenuifolia

Height and spread
12x7cm/5x3in

Temperature
13–24°C/55–75°F

Position
Bright light

Flowering time
Spring

Originating in the tropical rainforests from Mexico to Costa Rica, *M. tenuifolia* is commonly grown for its coconut-scented flowers, whose aroma is strongest in the early morning. The 5cm/2in flowers are triangular, and a deep mahogany-brown, with pale yellow lips densely spotted in russet. It has a straggling habit, with the short rhizomes enclosed in brown scales connecting each small, egg-shaped pseudobulb, from which grow long, thin, grass-like leaves.

–

WHERE TO GROW

Grow in a pot or basket (see Growing orchids in a basket, page 84) or mount on tree fern (see Mounting orchids on bark, page 94) in an intermediate greenhouse or on a windowsill. *Maxillaria tenuifolia* enjoys bright light and a humid environment.

HOW TO GROW

Keep moist to replicate its native habitat of thick humus mats that accumulate on the branches of trees.

GROWING TIP

Plants growing mounted on bark or tree fern require more frequent watering that those planted in pots or baskets.

FLORAL FRAGRANCES
Numerous orchid species are grown for their perfumes, including the heavily scented *Coelogyne nitida* (aka *C. ochracea*) and the Cuban *Encyclia phoenicea*, which gives off the aroma of chocolate or vanilla.

Mounting orchids on bark

Pieces of cork-oak bark make an ideal substrate for mounting orchids on another piece of bark, a short branch or a twig of a tree such as apple, or on a piece of tree fern. The bark is harvested sustainably in south-west Europe and north-west Africa from managed forests of cork oak (*Quercus suber*). It is light, impermeable, has a rough surface to which orchid roots can adhere, and it will last for many years. Cork-oak bark is also full of cracks and crevices. Initially, attach the plant to the bark using galvanized or plastic-coated wire or, for a smaller specimen, nylon fishing line. Eventually, the orchid roots will adhere firmly to the mount, and the wire will no longer be needed. Alternatively, attach the plant using soft string, which will eventually rot.

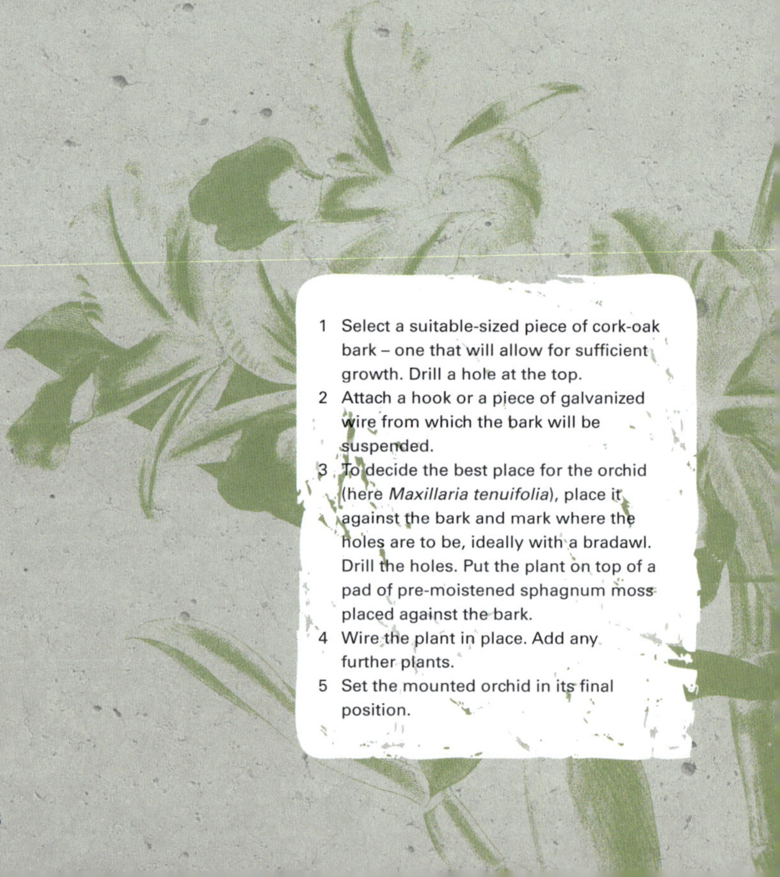

1. Select a suitable-sized piece of cork-oak bark – one that will allow for sufficient growth. Drill a hole at the top.
2. Attach a hook or a piece of galvanized wire from which the bark will be suspended.
3. To decide the best place for the orchid (here *Maxillaria tenuifolia*), place it against the bark and mark where the holes are to be, ideally with a bradawl. Drill the holes. Put the plant on top of a pad of pre-moistened sphagnum moss placed against the bark.
4. Wire the plant in place. Add any further plants.
5. Set the mounted orchid in its final position.

1

2

3

5

4

Pansy orchid

Miltonia spectabilis

Height and spread
35x25cm/14x10in

Temperature
13–24°C/55–75°F

Position
Summer shade

Flowering time
Summer

The nine species of *Miltonia* from Brazil and Peru are popularly called pansy orchids (see also Colombian pink pansy orchid, page 97). They have large flat flowers, with a satin texture, which can last 6–8 weeks. Their perfume is particularly strong around midday.

—

WHERE TO GROW

Grow in a warm humid greenhouse or on a windowsill on a tray of moist gravel or expanded clay granules, to create a humid micro-environment.

HOW TO GROW

This spectacular orchid has a sprawling habit that is best accommodated in a wide, shallow pot or basket (see Growing orchids in a basket, page 84) in a mixture of two parts fine- or medium-grade bark, one part sphagnum moss and one part perlite, which allows plenty of drainage. Do not let the compost dry out completely. Overwatering, however, can also be harmful, leading to rotting of the pseudobulbs.

GROWING TIP

Crinkling or concertina leaves can be caused by overwatering or underwatering, and provides an early indication that the watering regime needs some attention. The state of the compost should be examined.

ANOTHER NOTABLE SPECIES

- *M. candida* is a sweetly scented species from Brazil. Individual flowers have a flared white lip with a purple blotch in the throat, and contrasting rich brown sepals and petals. A well-grown specimen can carry as many as ten large blooms on a single spike.

A MAGNIFICENT SIGHT

In 1856 a specimen of *M. spectabilis* 4.5m/15ft in circumference was exhibited at Glasgow Botanic Gardens.

Colombian pink pansy orchid

Miltoniopsis vexillaria

Miltoniopsis literally means 'resembling a *Miltonia*' – the other pansy orchid (see page 96). The six *Miltoniopsis* species occur in the Andean cloud forests from Colombia to Peru. Colombian pink pansy orchid produces long sprays of beautiful, large, flat, pale lavender blooms, with lemon centres, offset by pale sage-green foliage atop flat, egg-shaped pseudobulbs.

—

Height and spread
35x20cm/14x8in

Temperature
13–24°C/55–75°F

Position
Shade

Flowering time
Autumn–winter

WHERE TO GROW

Grow in an intermediate greenhouse or on a windowsill with some shading.

HOW TO GROW

Needs a mixture of two parts fine-grade bark, one part perlite and one part sphagnum moss. Keep the compost evenly moist, but not wet, as this can lead to rotting of the thin white roots and pseudobulbs.

BEAUTIFUL HYBRIDS
Breeders have used the attractive waterfall pattern on the lip of *M. phalaenopsis* to produce a range of lovely windowsill plants.

GROWING TIP

Use fertilizer at one-quarter or half-strength during the growing period, alternating with a thorough flushing of the compost with rainwater in between feeding every second watering.

Princess Alexandra's oncidium

Oncidium alexandrae aka *Odontoglossum crispum*

Numerous large, crystalline-white flowers with crimped petals, often flushed with purple on the reverses and beautifully marked with spots and blotches, are carried on long, sometimes branching spikes. In the nineteenth century, at the height of 'orchid fever' (see A little history, page 9), Princess Alexandra's oncidium was collected and imported into the UK by the hundreds of thousands. To obtain these plants, tens of thousands of trees were cut down. Today, the remnant populations are endangered.

–

Height and spread
35x35cm/14x14in

Temperature
10–24°C/50–75°F

Position
Shade

Flowering time
Year-round

WHERE TO GROW

Grow in a cool, humid and shady environment to match the native habitat of the cloud forests of Colombia. As well as in the cool greenhouse, with care Princess Alexandra's oncidium can be grown on an east- or west-facing windowsill.

THE WORLD'S MOST EXPENSIVE ORCHID

In 1886 Baron Schröder paid 160 guineas (around £22,500 today) for a particularly fine variety of Princess Alexandra's oncidium.

HOW TO GROW

Plant in a free-draining, moisture-retentive compost mix of two parts fine-grade bark, one part sphagnum moss and one part perlite. Use a balanced fertilizer at half-strength throughout the summer growing period, alternating feeding with rainwater. To display the flower spikes to their best advantage see Training flower spikes, page 102. Repot young plants and those not producing flower spikes in spring. Repot flowering-sized plants in autumn.

GROWING TIP

When grown well, each new pseudobulb of Princess Alexandra's oncidium will increase in size each year, until the pseudobulbs reach the size of small apples.

Oncidium ornithorhynchum

Height and spread
12x15cm/5x6in

Temperature
13–24°C/55–75°F

Position
Light shade

Flowering time
Autumn–winter

Whereas *Oncidium* usually bears yellow and brown flowers, this easy and free-flowering species, found growing from Mexico to Colombia, produces long branching sprays of large numbers of small, rose-purple flowers, each with a contrasting yellow crest. They emit a delicious sweet perfume reminiscent of sherbet. Smooth, light green pseudobulbs each have a pair of narrow leaves on this compact plant.

—

WHERE TO GROW

Grow in an intermediate greenhouse, or on a windowsill, with a little summer shade.

HOW TO GROW

Plant in a free-draining mixture of two parts medium-grade pine bark, one part perlite and one part sphagnum moss. Maintain a moist atmosphere throughout the year. Water well and feed every third watering with half-strength fertilizer in the growing season, allowing the compost to dry out between waterings.

GROWING TIP

Needs a winter rest, so give only sufficient water to prevent the compost drying out completely. Overwatering at this time can lead to rotting of the pseudobulbs.

ANOTHER NOTABLE SPECIES

- *Gomesa croesus* (aka *Oncidium croesus*) is another delightful dwarf species suitable for windowsill culture. Each raceme carries up to six reddish brown flowers, with contrasting yellow lips, each with a central, dark purple blotch.

Bee orchid

Ophrys apifera

Height and spread	15x7cm/6x3in
Temperature	–10–24°C/14–75°F
Position	Full sun to light shade
Flowering time	Summer

The flowers of bee orchid resemble insects and, despite the diminutive stature, are every bit as exotic as anything found in the tropics. This orchid is adapted to surviving long, hot, dry summers – its green rosettes of leaves appearing above ground in autumn and dying down in summer.

–

WHERE TO GROW

These plants of calcareous (slightly alkaline) soils occur naturally in full sun or partial shade. Grow in a pot in a frost-free greenhouse or a cold frame, or in a plunge bed (see Growing orchids in a cold greenhouse or cold frame, page 20). Burying a (preferably terracotta) pot in a bed of moist sand helps maintain a constant temperature and moisture content. Alternatively, construct a special raised bed in the garden.

HOW TO GROW

In late summer or early autumn, plant tubers in fresh, free-draining, neutral to slightly alkaline, soil-based compost. A number of recipes for composts for *Ophrys* species are available, incorporating a wide range of constituents; however, a mixture of two parts calcarious (>pH 7) or neutral loam and one part horticultural sand is adequate for *O. apifera*.

GROWING TIP

Once the leaves have died down, dig up the small oval tubers, clean them by removing any compost and store the dry tubers somewhere cool and dark in a plastic bag.

SEXUAL DECEIT

Ophrys species typically mimic female bees and produce pheromones that attract male bees, which attempt to mate with the flowers – an activity referred to as pseudo-copulation. *Ophrys apifera* is unusual in that, in the UK, it is self-pollinating.

Asian slipper orchid

Paphiopedilum niveum

Height and spread
5x15cm/2x6in

Temperature
13–24°C/55–75°F

Position
Light shade

Flowering time
Spring–summer

This charming little slipper orchid from Thailand, Malaysia and Borneo produces fans of narrow, dark green leaves patterned with paler tessellations, and with purple-spotted undersides. As the snow-white flowers open atop a 15cm/6in stem, the pouches (lips) are like little eggs, nestling beneath a lemon-yellow staminode. To display the pendent flowers to their best advantage see Training flower spikes, page 102.

—

WHERE TO GROW

Originating in north-east India, Asian slipper orchid is one of the easiest slipper orchids to cultivate. Grow it in a cool greenhouse or on a windowsill in light shade.

HOW TO GROW

Add a few limestone chippings to a compost mix of two parts pine bark, one part sphagnum moss and one part perlite, to mimic the pockets of humus in limestone crevices in its natural habitat. To avoid crown rot, water (and feed) by immersing the pot up to its rim in a container of rainwater. Feed with a half-strength balanced fertilizer throughout the growing period. Reduce watering in winter, keeping the compost moist, but not wet.

GROWING TIP

As a general rule, slipper orchids with mottled leaves require warmer conditions than those with plain leaves such as Asian slipper orchid (*P. insigne*).

A NOTABLE HYBRID

- *P.* Maudiae is a relatively easy slipper orchid to grow and so is commonly offered for sale in garden centres. It has long-lasting flowers, with apple-green lips and large, white, striped dorsal sepals, and attractive, boldly mottled, dark and light green leaves.

Training flower spikes

To display the flowers to their best advantage, either for your own personal enjoyment or for an orchid show, the stems of many orchids will benefit from being tied to a suitable supporting cane, which should be hidden as far as possible. Moth orchids (*Phalaenopsis*), cymbidiums and oncidiums, for example, typically produce tall spikes carrying large numbers of blooms. Oncidiums often develop stems with many branches. Canes can be gently inserted (it helps if they each have a pointed end) into the compost alongside the newly emerging flower spikes, taking care not to damage any new shoots or roots. Then tie each flower spike to its cane with soft string, raffia or plastic clips. Place a protective cap on the end of each cane.

If an arching spray is preferred, a length of plastic-coated or galvanized wire can be inserted into the top of a hollow cane, and bent to form the required shape. Especially where plants are growing on a windowsill, the flower spikes will grow towards the light source. Plants can either be kept in the same orientation, or turned regularly, to avoid a wiggly stem. Trim the cane (taking care not to damage the flower spike) once the spike has ceased growing. Then replace the protective cap.

The flowering stems of many paphiopedilums tend to droop, and each can be tied to a thin cane.

A As flowering spikes of moth orchids develop, and the flowers open, tie each stem to a supporting cane and place a protective cap on top of it.

B Special clips can be used to tie the flowering spike of a moth orchid to a bent wire support.

C Support the tall flowering canes of dendrobium hybrids by tying them to a cane, with soft string.

D The flowering stems of a moth orchid such as this artificially coloured one can be trained to form an attractive arch.

E To achieve this stunning effect, carefully train flowering stems (here moth orchid) before the flowers develop, while they are still flexible.

A

B

C

D

E

Moth orchid

Phalaenopsis

Moth orchid is the ideal beginner's orchid. It has bright green, stiff, ovoid, leathery leaves and flowers throughout the year on upright or arching spikes, 50cm/20in or more long. Its numerous round blooms are borne in colours from white to yellow to deep burgundy; some have spots or stripes. They remain in flower for weeks, or even months at a time. A range of pretty miniature moth orchids is also available and suitable for windowsill culture and for growing in a terrarium (see Planting up a terrarium, page 116).

Height and spread
20x35cm/8–14in

Temperature
13–24°C/55–75°F

Position
Summer shade

Flowering time
Year-round

–

WHERE TO GROW

Grow on a windowsill in a bright, well-lit position while avoiding full sunlight, which can scorch the leaves. Moth orchids also thrive in an intermediate or warm greenhouse (see *Phalaenopsis schilleriana*, page 106), as well as in a terrarium.

SOURCE OF MUCH BEAUTY

Phalaenopsis amabilis is found in the parentage of all the lovely moth orchids on sale in garden centres and supermarkets around the world. It is the embodiment of floral sophistication, with its large (10cm/4in), rounded, snow-white blooms on long, arching, sometimes branching inflorescences.

Phalaenopsis amabilis

HOW TO GROW

Pot in a medium-grade bark. Water once a week when moth orchid is actively growing, by immersing the pot in tepid water for 10–15 minutes. Then remove any water in the crown of the plant, to prevent rot setting in. Never overwater. Spray moth orchid roots regularly in hot weather. Reduce watering in winter. To display the flower spikes to their best advantage see Training flower spikes, page 102. Once your plant has finished flowering, remove the flower spike close to its base or, if the plant is robust, cut at a point two or three nodes up from the base (see Looking after your moth orchid once flowered, page 33). Repot every two years, in spring, positioning the plant in the middle of the pot, as it is monopodial. Moth orchid flowers are relatively easy to pollinate (see Pollinating orchids, page 124).

BE ALERT

Mealybugs can sometimes be found in the crown of the plant; remove them at once (see Pests, page 135). If the atmosphere is too humid (a potential problem for plants growing in a greenhouse), moth orchid flowers may develop dark fungal spots (see Fungal spotting on flowers, page 137).

GROWING TIP

If a plant fails to flower again, try moving it to a cooler (not cold) location. Alternatively, if the leaves are soft and dark green, your plant may need a little more light. Well-grown plants have quite rigid leaves.

Phalaenopsis schilleriana

Height and spread
15x10cm/6x4in

Temperature
15–24°C/59–75°F

Position
Summer shade

Flowering time
Winter

With its drooping, dark green leaves, mottled with silver-grey and purple undersides, *P. schilleriana* from the Philippines is worth growing for its foliage alone. However, this characteristic, coupled with long branching sprays of one hundred or more of soft violet-pink flowers on a well-grown plant, makes it a real showstopper.

—

WHERE TO GROW

Grow in a warm greenhouse with a relative humidity of around 80 per cent.

HOW TO GROW

Plant in medium-grade pine bark. Water weekly when actively growing, or more frequently if the compost becomes dry (see Moth orchid, page 105). Although *P. schilleriana* enjoys a winter rest, the compost should not dry out completely and leaves should not be allowed to desiccate. Feed regularly during the growing period with half-strength fertilizer. Remove or shorten the flower spike after flowering (see Looking after your moth orchid once flowered, page 33).

GROWING TIP

In order to induce flowering, plants require cooler night-time temperatures in autumn.

OTHER NOTABLE SPECIES

- *P. equestris* is a charming miniature species that produces sprays of white or pink-suffused flowers. It has been used in the breeding of smaller multiflowered hybrids, and is also well worth growing in its own right.
- *P. violacea* carries a short inflorescence of 3–5 fragrant flowers, with small lips and pointed ivory petals and sepals with suffused violet centres.

South American slipper orchid

Phragmipedium longifolium

South American slipper orchid is found from Costa Rica to Ecuador growing on steep banks in running water, often by rivers, where its roots are constantly wet and well-aerated. It has long, strap-like leaves and large, olive-green and caramel flowers that are borne sequentially along the flower spike. Individual blooms drop off as they age and new ones form at the tip.

Height and spread
30x30cm/12x12in

Temperature
13–24°C/55–75°F

Position
Light shade

Flowering time
Autumn

WHERE TO GROW

Grow in an intermediate greenhouse or on a windowsill.

HOW TO GROW

Plant in rock wool (wearing a protective mask and gloves; see Rock wool, page 27), or in a mixture of equal parts bark and perlite. Water from the top. In summer, add one-quarter strength balanced fertilizer once a week, changing to similar strength tomato fertilizer in autumn. Flush the compost through with rainwater every third watering. Fertilize once a month at other times of the year.

GROWING TIP

Keep the roots constantly moist by standing the pot in a saucer of water.

A NOTABLE HYBRID

- *P.* Sedenii is a vigorous and attractive hybrid of *P. schlimii* and *P. longifolium.* It has off-white sepals and petals and rose-pink pouches.

Making a corsage

YOU WILL NEED

- Vase filled with water
- Kitchen paper to remove moisture from flower stem
- Hobby wire, green lacquered 'stub wires' 22 gauge (0.64mm diameter, 25cm/10in long)
- Wire cutters
- White waterproof florists' tape
- Scissors
- Hobby wire, 'silvered rose wire' 32 gauge (0.20mm diameter, 18cm/7in long)
- Ribbons, assorted varieties and colours
- Green waterproof florists' tape (optional)
- Pearl-headed long pins for securing to outfit

At one time big showy cattleya were popular as corsages, and enormous numbers of *C. trianae* were taken from the wild and imported into the USA for the cut flower industry. Today, you are more likely to see a phalaenopsis, cymbidium or dendrobium – the so-called Singapore orchids available from florists. A bridal bouquet is an obvious choice for such special blooms, but there is also a return to the use of corsages for all kinds of special events: these are worn not only on clothing but also on the wrist, in the hair, attached to a clutch bag or even a book.

Select flowers and ribbons to complement the outfit being worn. Gather together the foliage to be used. Some leaves are more robust than others: for example, camellia, rhododendron or gardenia are invaluable. For a lighter style, ivy (*Hedera*) and rose leaves may be preferred. Choose an odd number of leaves of differing sizes.

A filler material may also be used for added interest. This could be maidenhair fern (*Adiantum*), asparagus fern (*Asparagus densiflorus*, *A. setaceus*) or gypsophila. Various interesting accessories are available.

Before you make the final item, it is a good idea to have a practice run using a less-than-perfect flower or flowers. Start by covering a tray with a soft towel ready to line up all the components.

1. Remove a flower together with its stem from the parent plant (here phalaenopsis). Place in water for at least thirty minutes.
2. Remove the flower from the vase and blot excess moisture with kitchen paper. Hold the flower stem firmly between your fingers, while slowly threading a green wire along the centre until the end of the wire goes just into the flower itself, but not right through to the column.
3. Take a piece of tape and cover the now wired stem, starting at the base of the flower, continuing down the stem and over the wire.
4. Cover the silver wire with the florists' tape, and bend into a hairpin. Take the prepared hairpin wire and carefully thread it through the gaps either side of the lip. Avoid damaging the sepals. Carefully bring the wires alongside the flower stem, and wrap one wire around the other and the stem. Cover with tape.
5. Wire all the other corsage items as shown, and line up ready for assembly.
6. For the final assembly, take a prepared leaf and one of the accessories, pressing the taped wires together gently to hold them in place. Add the orchid, followed by additional leaves on either side. Adjust the composition until you are happy with the result.
7. Finally fasten the ribbon bow by wrapping its wire around the other components to secure it in place. Neaten off with tape, and the corsage is ready to be worn or given as a gift. Remember to include the fancy pearl pins for attachment.

1

2

3

4

5

6

7

Pleione formosana

Height and spread
10x15cm/4x6in

Temperature
5–24°C/41–75°F

Position
Dappled shade

Flowering time
Spring

A single, delicate, pale violet flower, with a frilly, funnel-shaped, white lip spotted with pale caramel, emerges from the base of each slightly conical pseudobulb in spring. As the flower dies down, a large pleated leaf develops.

–

WHERE TO GROW

Grow in a frost-free greenhouse or on a windowsill. Pots can be transferred to a shady spot in the garden in summer.

HOW TO GROW

Each spring, before the roots begin to emerge, pot the pseudobulbs in fresh compost of equal parts medium-grade bark, sphagnum moss and perlite, preferably in a terracotta pan or half-pot. Although the pseudobulbs can be planted in individual pots, a pan containing a number of pseudobulbs of the same variety is particularly attractive when in flower. Once the leaves have fallen in autumn, clean and store the pseudobulbs in a cool (but not freezing) space in a plastic bag over winter.

GROWING TIP

In spring, keep the compost slightly moist until the first roots are more than 1cm/½in long – otherwise the roots can die, and fresh roots will not emerge. Once the roots have developed, fertilize with a balanced fertilizer throughout the summer growth period, flushing the compost through with rainwater every third or fourth watering.

IN THE GARDEN

In frost-free districts, as long as each pseudobulb is buried a few centimetres below the surface of the compost, species such as *P. limprichtii* can be grown outdoors in the garden, in a specially constructed raised bed.

EPIPHYTE, SYMPODIAL

Cockleshell orchid

Prosthechea cochleata aka black orchid, clamshell orchid, octopus orchid

Found in countries bordering the Caribbean, this orchid is easily recognizable with its upside-down flowers displaying shell-like lips bordered in deep purple. Long, narrow, twisted, pale green sepals and petals dangle below each lip, like tentacles. An inflorescence, 35cm/14in long, can produce up to twenty flowers.

—

Height and spread
50x25cm/20x10in

Temperature
13–24°C/55–75°F

Position
Light shade

Flowering time
Year-round

WHERE TO GROW

Grow in an intermediate greenhouse or on a windowsill.

HOW TO GROW

Plant the large, slightly stalked, flask-shaped pseudobulbs in a pot containing a medium-grade bark compost. Maintain a moist atmosphere throughout the year. Water year-round, using a quarter-strength balanced fertilizer, flushing the compost through with rainwater every third watering.

GROWING TIP

This orchid does not require a winter rest.

ANOTHER MOLLUSC
In Belize, where cockleshell orchid is the national flower, it is also known locally either as black orchid (because of the deep purple border around the flowers' lips) or rather appropriately, because Belize is famous for its beautiful coral reefs, as octopus orchid.

Butterfly orchid

Psychopsis krameriana

With their narrow antennae and broad, pale yellow lips with margins of cinnamon spots, all borne at the tips of long spindly flower stems, the fantastic flowers of butterfly orchids resemble exotic insects trembling in a tropical breeze Each short, flattened pseudobulb bears a single thick, rigid, leathery, dark green leaf with red-brown mottling.

Height and spread
30x15cm/12x6in

Temperature
15–32°C/59–90°F

Position
Light shade

Flowering time
Year-round

—

WHERE TO GROW

Grow in an intermediate or warm greenhouse, with a relative humidity of 80 per cent and plenty of air movement, to replicate butterfly orchid's native habitat of tropical lowlands and lower montane rainforests in South and Central America.

HOW TO GROW

Mount on a pad of sphagnum moss on a piece of bark (see Mounting orchids on bark, page 94) or grow in a basket (see Growing orchids in a basket, page 84). Butterfly orchid can also be planted in a terracotta pot. Use a half-strength balanced fertilizer throughout the year, with a thorough watering of rainwater every third watering, allowing the medium to dry out in between watering.

GROWING TIP

Butterfly orchid continues to produce a series of flowers in succession, and can remain in flower for many months, so refrain from cutting the flower spike. It sometimes produces keikis on the flowering stem (see Keikis, page 36).

RELATED SPECIES
Closely related *Psychopsis papilio* is very similar in appearance to butterfly orchid, but has larger flowers.

Blunt greenhood

Pterostylis curta

Blunt greenhood grows in moist woodland and grassy habitats in eastern Australia. A single quirky flower emerges in spring from the centre of each rosette of leaves; it has dorsal sepals and petals fused to form the characteristic 'hood'. A tongue-like lip is located in a 'V' formed by the two remaining sepals, and it springs back when gently stroked.

Height and spread
15x10cm/6x4in

Temperature
5–24°C/41–75°F

Position
Light shade

Flowering time
Spring

WHERE TO GROW

Grow in a frost-free greenhouse or on cool windowsill.

HOW TO GROW

Being summer-dormant, blunt greenhood's leaves die down after flowering. Repot annually: sieve the old compost to find the tiny round tubers. Pot them in a mixture of two parts loam, one part perlite or grit, and one part leafmould, with the addition of a little blood, fish and bone fertilizer, spacing the tubers evenly. Cover with a thin layer of soil plus a layer of chopped pine, spruce or larch needles, to deter slugs and snails (see Pests, page 136). Water weekly once the new leaves begin to emerge.

GROWING TIP

Blunt greenhoods multiply rapidly by tuber offsets, and after a few seasons can fill a shallow pan.

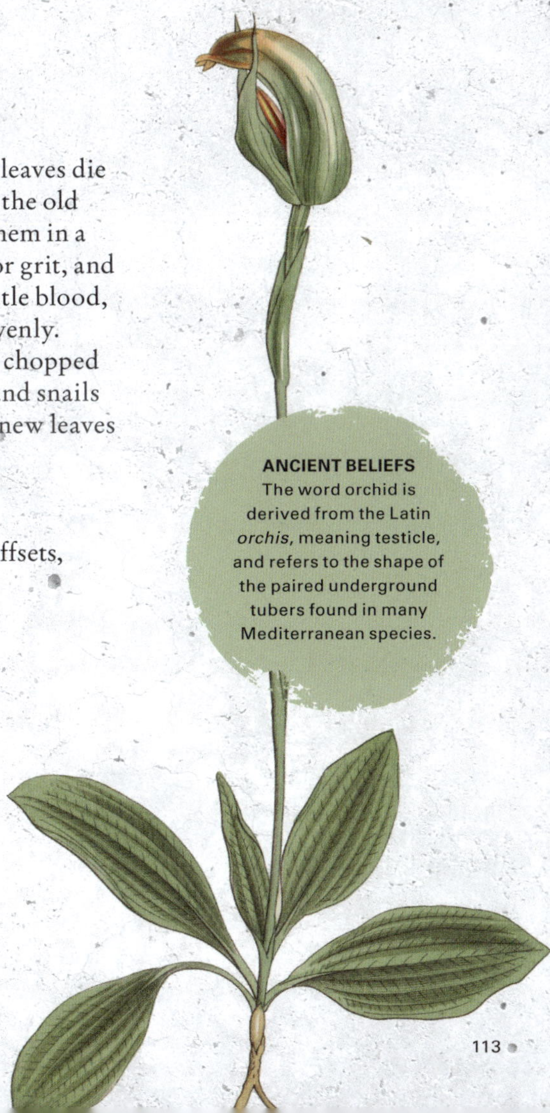

ANCIENT BELIEFS
The word orchid is derived from the Latin *orchis*, meaning testicle, and refers to the shape of the paired underground tubers found in many Mediterranean species.

Restrepia striata

Restrepia striata is a small compact plant with leathery, slightly heart-shaped leaves borne on slender stalks. What appears to be the flower's lip is, in fact, the two lateral sepals fused to form a 4cm/1½in tongue, which is attractively striped. The petals resemble antennae.

—

WHERE TO GROW

Grow in a cool greenhouse or a terrarium (see Planting up a terrarium, page 116), to match the cool mountain cloud forests, where this species originates.

HOW TO GROW

Grow in a small pot or basket in sphagnum moss with the addition of a little perlite (see Growing orchids in a basket, page 84). Keep the sphagnum moist but not wet, and renew it annually. Alternatively, grow *R. striata* on a tree fern slab, where its fine roots will cling to the tree fern support (see Mounting orchids on bark, page 94). Give plants an early-morning spray with rainwater. An additional light spray in late evening in warm summer weather is beneficial.

GROWING TIP

Restrepia striata often produces keikis, which can potted up individually (see Keikis, page 36), or it can be propagated by leaf cuttings (see Cuttings, page 37).

Restrepia cuprea

Height and spread
10x30cm/4x12in

Temperature
10–24°C/50–75°F

Position
Dappled shade

Flowering time
Year-round

TINY POLLINATORS
In their natural habitat, the flowers of restrepias are pollinated by minute fungus gnats

Foxtail orchid

Rhynchostylis retusa

Height and spread
40x20cm/16x8in
Temperature
13–24°C/55–75°F
Position
Light summer shade
Flowering time
Summer

In foxtail orchid's tropical Asian home, fans of robust fleshy leaves on short stout stems cling to their tree hosts by thick aerial roots. Pendent racemes, 15–40cm/6–16in long, arch downwards from the leaf axils, bearing large numbers of closely packed and strongly fragrant, small, amethyst-spotted, waxy, white flowers, with contrasting amethyst-purple lips, which can last up to six weeks.

–

WHERE TO GROW

Grow in an intermediate or warm greenhouse.

HOW TO GROW

Plant in a basket (see Growing orchids in a basket, page 84) or mount on a piece of cork oak (see Mounting orchids on bark, page 94) because foxtail orchid roots appreciate the freedom to roam and should not be confined to a pot. When the roots have active green tips, use rainwater to water or spray roots once or twice daily, depending on the weather conditions. Use half-strength fertilizer weekly when the roots are growing.

GROWING TIP

Foxtail orchid appreciates a high relative humidity (80 per cent or more) and good air movement.

OTHER NOTABLE SPECIES

- *R. gigantea* has larger, more boldly marked flowers borne on shorter racemes in winter.

Planting up a terrarium

Not everyone has a garden and, even if they do, not everyone has space for a greenhouse. This, coupled with ever-higher heating bills, has led to an increasing number of people growing their plants indoors, either in a basement, on the windowsill or in a terrarium. The advantages of a terrarium include the ability to maintain a humid environment and a stable temperature. If you choose to incorporate additional lighting, this can eliminate any problems of insufficient daylight, particularly in winter months. However, you should avoid placing your terrarium in direct sunlight, as your mini-greenhouse will retain too much heat.

A terrarium can make an attractive feature in a room. Although you can purchase specially made items, incorporating lights and fans, it is possible to construct your own terrarium from an aquarium tank or other glass container, or to grow plants under a bell jar. You are limited only by your imagination. Such a mini-garden will be low maintenance – the only requirement being to mist the plants from time to time with rainwater (not tap water, to avoid any build-up of salts).

Your choice of plants will depend on the size of the terrarium (see above right). They can be planted in pots, which are then disguised by moss; epiphytes such as lepanthes can be attached to a branch or piece of driftwood.

To make an attractive display include small-growing non-orchid plants with attractive foliage (see below right).

It is important, before you purchase your terrarium, that you ascertain whether or not it is watertight. Many modern versions are very attractive, but may not be hold water efficiently.

ORCHID PLANTS FOR A TERRARIUM

Lepanthes
Masdevallia
Miniature moth orchid (*Phalaenopsis*; small, multiflowered)
Restrepia
Stelis

SMALL-GROWING NON-ORCHIDACEOUS PLANTS FOR A TERRARIUM

Begonia (small-leaved)
Button fern (*Pellaea rotundifolia*)
Delta maidenhair fern (*Adiantum raddianum*)
Mosaic plant (*Fittonia albivenis* Verschaffeltii Group)
Pilea
Polka dot plant (*Hypoestes phyllostachya*)
Radiator plant (*Peperomia caperata*)
Selaginella

1. Clean the glass of the terrarium thoroughly, to allow for maximum light.
2. Place a layer of washed horticultural gravel or stones on the bottom of the terrarium.
3. Add a further layer of moist sphagnum moss.
4. Insert a plant (here polka dot plant/*Hypoestes phyllostachya*).
5. Then add further ones (here a miniature moth orchid) to make an attractive display. Add a little more water, then close the top of the terrarium and set it in a suitable position.

Sarcochilus hartmannii

Height and spread
15x12cm/6x5in

Temperature
13–24°C/55–75°F

Position
Light summer shade

Flowering time
Winter–spring

A popular eastern Australian endemic, *S. hartmannii* produces erect, slightly arching sprays of up to twenty-five white flowers, 1–4cm/½–1½in across, with red spotting in each centre. Fans of thick, channelled, dark green leaves on branching stems form clumps on boulders and cliffs in *S. hartmannii*'s natural habitat, where it roots in mats of humus. When crossed with *S. fitzgeraldii* it produces the vigorous and floriferous hybrid *S.* Fitzhart.

–

WHERE TO GROW

Grow in an intermediate or cool greenhouse or on a windowsill. *Sarcochilus hartmannii* appreciates a humid environment and a cool root run. In the home, a humid micro-environment can be produced by standing pots on a tray containing moistened gravel.

HOW TO GROW

Its compact nature makes *S. hartmannii* ideal for growing in a shallow pan, pot or basket (see Growing orchids in a basket, page 84). Keep the compost moist rather than wet. If the leaves begin to show signs of shrivelling, this may indicate a lack of water, but do check to ensure that a lack of roots is not the problem.

GROWING TIP

Do not allow water to remain in the leaf axils, especially in the cool winter months, as this can cause a fatal rot to set in.

ORCHID ICE CREAM
In Turkey, orchid tubers are harvested to make *salep*, a constituent of a regional ice cream, dondurma.

Sobralia macrantha

Height and spread
100x35cm/39x14in
Temperature
13–24°C/55–75°F
Position
Summer shade
Flowering time
Summer

Widely cultivated in Mexico for its beautiful, large, papery, magenta flowers, *S. macrantha* is a real showstopper. Although individual flowers last for only two or three days (in Spanish it is called *la flor de un día*), each individual bamboo-like cane produces two flowers in succession, and a large plant with many canes can remain in flower for a number of weeks.

—

WHERE TO GROW

Grow in an intermediate greenhouse or large conservatory.

HOW TO GROW

Plant in a large plastic container, with plenty of drainage, in coarse-grade bark. Commence watering and feeding with half-strength balanced fertilizer in spring, when the thick roots become active. Reduce watering in winter, keeping the compost just moist.

GROWING TIP

Does best if left undisturbed for some years before being repotted.

EXOTIC ROADSIDE WEEDS

Sobralia is a genus of 30–50 species from Central America and tropical South America. Although some species are epiphytic, *Sobralia* is typically terrestrial, with large masses often seen in flower on steep slopes and by roadsides.

Stanhopea tigrina

Height and spread
25x25cm/10x10in
Temperature
13–24°C/55–75°F
Position
Light shade
Flowering time
Summer–autumn

This spectacular Mexican orchid boasts heavily perfumed, large, fleshy, pendent, creamy yellow flowers marked with brown-purple spots. They open with a distinct 'pop'. The pseudobulbs have broad, ribbed, dark green leaves.

–

WHERE TO GROW

Grow in an intermediate greenhouse suspended in a slatted, wooden or wire basket (see Growing orchids in a basket, page 84) in equal parts medium-grade pine bark and sphagnum moss. Such a position will display the flowers best as they emerge from the base of the pseudobulb and hang downwards.

HOW TO GROW

Being native to seasonally wet forests, *S. tigrina* needs copious amounts of water in the growing season, as well as a humid environment. Gradually reduce watering in autumn, without allowing the compost to dry out completely.

GROWING TIP

Give *S. tigrina* a light spray with rainwater during its winter rest.

BEE AFTERSHAVE

Many neotropical epiphytic orchids are pollinated by male euglossine bees, which collect the flowers' perfume, inadvertently pollinating them in the process. The males then use the scent to attract female bees.

Stelis emarginata

Height and spread
23x30cm/9x12in

Temperature
10–24°C/50–75°F

Position
Shade

Flowering time
Spring

With around 500 species, *Stelis* is immediately recognizable by its rows of small triangular flowers on long stems. Many species are sensitive to light levels, opening in the daytime and closing at night. What appear to be petals are sepals – the petals being reduced to tiny structures in the centre of each flower. *Stelis emarginata* grows in cloud forests from Mexico to Peru. It sports rows of bright orange flowers, which emerge from a sheath at the base of each long, thick, spatulate leaf.

–

WHERE TO GROW

Grow in a humid cool greenhouse in shade or in a terrarium (see Planting up a terrarium, page 116).

HOW TO GROW

Pot in a moisture-retentive but free-draining compost such as a mixture of equal parts sphagnum moss, perlite and fine-grade bark. Keep the compost evenly moist year-round.

GROWING TIP

Stelis emarginata will grow throughout the year, and does not require a winter rest from watering.

ALL GREEK TO ME
The name *Stelis* is derived from the Greek word for mistletoe, referring to the plant's epiphytic habit.

Stenoglottis fimbriata

Height and spread
20x25cm/8x10in

Temperature
5–24°C/41–75°F

Position
Dappled shade

Flowering time
Autumn

This very desirable South African orchid produces an erect inflorescence of up to thirty small, pretty, pale lilac flowers with distinctive, trilobed, spotted lips. They gradually open from the base towards the tip, and last several weeks. The blooms emerge from the centre of a horizontal rosette of long, spirally arranged, wavy margined, attractive, purple-spotted leaves.

—

WHERE TO GROW

Grow in a cool or intermediate greenhouse or on a windowsill.

HOW TO GROW

In spring, plant the elongated, fleshy tubers in a mixture of equal parts loam, beech leafmould and perlite, which will reflect the mossy substrates in *S. fimbriata*'s native habitat.

GROWING TIP

Allow *S. fimbriata* to dry after the leaves have died down as it becomes dormant after flowering.

MEDICINAL USE
Preparations made from the leaves of *S. fimbriata* are given in Africa as an enema to relieve flatulence.

Vanda ampullacea

aka *Ascocentrum ampullaceum*

This is a compact and charming Asian miniature orchid. Fans of dark green leaves produce tight clusters of vibrant red flowers, which emerge from the leaf axils. A well-grown specimen can almost disappear beneath an exuberant floral display.

—

Height and spread
20x15cm/8x6in

Temperature
13–24°C/55–75°F

Position
Light shade

Flowering time
Spring–summer

WHERE TO GROW

Grow in an intermediate greenhouse, with sufficient shade to prevent leaf burn. Its compact habit also makes *V. ampullacea* suitable for growing on a windowsill or under lights in a basement or cellar.

HOW TO GROW

Grow mounted (see Mounting orchids on bark, page 94) or in a basket (see Growing orchids in a basket, page 84). The thick silvery roots will cling tightly to the support or dangle into the humid atmosphere. Water and fertilize regularly in spring and summer, while the roots are actively growing. Reduce watering and cease fertilizing in autumn and winter.

GROWING TIP

In bright light the leaves of *V. ampullacea* become speckled with purple spots; give the plant some light shade if this happens, even though such spotting is not generally harmful to the plant.

AN ANCIENT LINEAGE
Fossilized bees preserved in amber with orchid pollen indicate that orchids belong to a surprisingly ancient family: their ancestors were around when dinosaurs roamed the Earth.

PROJECT 12

Pollinating orchids

Many rare and beautiful orchid species are becoming increasingly difficult to obtain. If they are to be maintained in cultivation, it is important to keep an eye out for those desirable plants, pollinate them, grow them from seed and share the resulting seedlings. Many are easy to pollinate. Moth orchids (*Phalaenopsis*) are good subjects with which to practise.

Ideally, flowers should be cross-pollinated (the pollen exchanged between two different clones). If the spike is made up of many flowers, pollinate a number of them. If successful, the ovary swells and becomes the seed capsule. Usually this takes place over a period of several months, depending on the species. If pollination results in the production of several seed capsules, to get the best-quality seed the number of capsules can be reduced over a period of time.

When mature, the capsule usually (but not always) changes colour from green to yellow before splitting and releasing a cloud of the seeds. Collect the seed just as the capsule begins to split, gathering it in a paper (never plastic) bag. Dry and store it in a paper envelope in a hermetically sealed container in a refrigerator at around 5°C (41°F) or in a freezer at –20°C (–4°F). If you do not intend germinating your own seed, post the seed to an orchid lab for germination. As long as it is kept dry and cool, seed of many orchid species will remain viable for many years.

1 Locate the pollen hidden behind the white anther cap at the end of the column (here of a moth orchid).
2 Gently remove the cap with a cocktail stick.
3 Locate the two clumps of bright yellow-orange pollen found inside.
4 Lift off the pollen attached to a sticky viscid disc, which will adhere to the cocktail stick.
5 Insert the pollen into the pool of viscous liquid that is the stigma. It is found underneath the column and just behind the anther cap.

Blue vanda

Vanda coerulea

The legendary, and increasingly rare, blue vanda from India and China has large, tessellated, long-lasting flowers borne on long racemes, which grow from the axils of fans of dark green leaves. A well-grown specimen, with fifty or more flowers, makes a spectacular sight. Early travellers wrote that it was occasionally subject to frost in its native hills.

–

Height and spread
100x30cm/39x12in

Temperature
10–24°C/50–75°F

Position
Light summer shade

Flowering time
Autumn–winter

WHERE TO GROW

Grow in a humid cool greenhouse.

HOW TO GROW

Plant in a basket containing large pieces of bark (see Mounting orchids on bark, page 94), as this orchid resents having its roots restricted. Water copiously and feed when the thick silvery roots are actively growing. Cut off the top of the plant, with its roots, and repot if the plant becomes too large.

GROWING TIP

Reduce watering in winter when root activity may be suspended; instead, just spray the roots lightly, according to the weather conditions.

TRUE BLUE
The flowers of blue vanda are very variable and always include a hint of lilac or pink. The only truly blue orchid is the Australian terrestrial species *Thelymitra crinita*.

Wind orchid

Vanda falcata aka *Neofinetia falcata*

Height and spread
15x15cm/6x6in

Temperature
13–24°C/55–75°F

Position
Medium shade

Flowering time
Summer

Native to China, Korea and Japan, wind orchid is especially loved in Japan, where it is exhibited in special pots and is called fuuran. It is appreciated as much for the shapes and variegations of the leaf fans as for its blooms. It easily produces side shoots and soon becomes a clump. Although typically seen with elegant, snow-white flowers, 2.5–3cm/1–1¼in across, with curved spurs, 4–6cm/1½–2½in long, there are also forms available in shades of pink or yellow. In the evenings and during the night the flowers give off a lovely, strong, sweet fragrance.

–

WHERE TO GROW

Grow in an intermediate greenhouse or on a windowsill.

HOW TO GROW

Plant in a small terracotta pot in lightly packed sphagnum moss (to allow plenty of air around the roots). Give a weekly quarter-strength feed during the summer growing period, and then once a month throughout the remainder of the year as long as the roots are active. Replace the compost each year.

GROWING TIP

Treat plants more like cacti – that is, do not overwater. It is important to maintain plenty of air around the roots.

ORCHID ROYALTY
In the Edo period in Japan only the elite were permitted to own wind orchids.

Vanilla orchid

Vanilla planifolia

Height and spread	5mx20cm/16ftx8in
Temperature	15–27°C/59–80°F
Position	Dappled shade
Flowering time	Year-round

Although vanilla is familiar as the world's most popular spice, people are often surprised to learn that its long dark pods, with their sticky black seeds, are the dried seed capsules of an orchid. Although there are more than one hundred vanilla species found growing around the globe, it is mainly *V. planifolia*, originally from Mexico and parts of Central America, that is cultivated in the tropics worldwide, but particularly in Madagascar, where, in the absence of its native pollinator, the yellow-green flowers are pollinated by hand.

—

WHERE TO GROW

Grow in a humid warm greenhouse, to replicate *V. planifolia*'s native habitat of lowland tropical forest. Unusually for orchids, vanillas have a climbing habit. The vines have alternating leaves, and eventually reach several metres in length in cultivation.

HOW TO GROW

Plant in a container with a free-draining medium- to coarse-grade pine bark compost, and train up a wire frame. Propagate by stem cuttings (see Cuttings, page 37).

GROWING TIP

Water and feed these thirsty plants regularly year-round.

ORNAMENTAL VANILLA

With its clusters of striking, pale green flowers with contrasting magenta lips, enormous specimens of *V. imperialis* are often grown as ornamentals in botanical gardens around the world. It is easier to flower than *V. planifolia*.

Zygopetalum mackayi

Height and spread
25x20cm/10x8in

Temperature
13–24°C/55–75°F

Position
Summer shade

Flowering time
Winter

This handsome, olive-green orchid is common in Brazil's Organ Mountains, where its large, egg-shaped pseudobulbs are crowned with three long, strap-like leaves. Erect spikes, to 75cm/30in long, each carry up to eight large, long-lasting flowers above the foliage. They give off a strong perfume reminiscent of hyacinths. The petals and sepals are pale green, with maroon spots and streaks that coalesce towards the tips, producing a stripy effect, while the broadly flared, white lips are each marked with a fan of purple-blue lines.

—

WHERE TO GROW

Grow in an intermediate greenhouse or on a windowsill, providing some summer shade to avoid burning the thin leaves.

HOW TO GROW

Plant in a pot filled with a free-draining compost of equal parts medium-grade bark, sphagnum moss and perlite. Give half-strength balanced fertilizer throughout the year, flushing the compost through with rainwater every fourth watering. Reduce watering when growth slows down in autumn.

GROWING TIP

Although *Z. mackayi* appreciates a humid environment, produced for example by growing on a tray of moist gravel, avoid allowing the foliage to remain wet overnight because unsightly spotting can result if temperatures are too low.

RECENT FINDS

New species are still being discovered – none, perhaps, more remarkable than the huge purple *Phragmipedium kovachii* in Peru in 2001, while scarlet *P. besseae* from Ecuador was first described in 1981.

NATIONAL
ORCHID
GARDEN
SINGAPORE
Happy
Singapore!

Where to see orchids

Orchids can be found in botanical gardens around the globe, and also closer to home. Some gardens have large collections that can be viewed by the general public, and many host annual orchid festivals that attract thousands of visitors each year. For those who enjoy travel, the opportunities to see orchids seem almost endless, and the following provide just a few examples of suitable destinations to whet your appetite. Singapore is a dream destination for orchid lovers, who will relish the Botanic Gardens, the Gardens by the Bay and the Bukit Timah Nature Reserve – one of the few remaining fragments of primary rainforest in the country.

Because of its varied topography, visitors to Costa Rica are able to find orchids growing in a wide range of different natural habitats in its national parks. At Lankester Botanical Garden you can learn more about the country's 1,450 species of orchid, before travelling to see them growing high in the tree canopy on specially constructed aerial walkways in the Monteverde Cloud Forest Reserve, or by taking a trip in a cable car at Braulio Carrillo National Park.

You may prefer to go on a pre-arranged tour, with a knowledgeable guide. These have the advantage that you are guaranteed to see orchids. Such tours are offered by a number of operators in South America, including in Ecuador and Peru. The mountains of the Andes are the hottest of hotspots when it comes to orchid diversity, while Colombia is home to an incredible 4,270 species of orchids. Visitors to China can see both temperate (*Cypripedium*) and tropical (*Paphiopedilum*) orchids in flower. A UNESCO World Heritage site, the stunningly beautiful Huanglong valley is home to thirty-four orchid species from twenty genera, including large populations of *Calypso bulbosa*, *Cypripedium tibeticum* and *C. flavum*. For those whose interest lies in discovering (and perhaps photographing) orchids in more temperate climes, there are companies that offer botanical tours around the Mediterranean.

OPPOSITE Botanic gardens around the world, such as this one in Singapore, often have wonderful orchid collections.

Visiting botanic gardens and orchid shows such as the Kew Orchid Festival (above) is an ideal way to buy plants, and to learn how to grow them from nursery people and other experienced growers.

Fortunately, even if you live in temperate zones, you do not have to travel to exotic locations to see orchids in their natural habitats. For example, the majority of the UK's population are probably unaware that there are around fifty-two species of orchid that can be seen around that country. Joining a local wildlife trust can provide the opportunity to visit a fragment of an English countryside once familiar to Charles Darwin himself. Such places are to be cherished.

This *Masdevallia rosea* was found growing by the side of the road in Ecuador. Sadly, the plant has since disappeared.

Orchid conservation

Sadly, many orchids, particularly the showier species, are teetering on the edge of extinction in the wild due to human activities. These include habitat destruction, global climate change and illegal collection for the horticultural trade. Many (perhaps most) species of *Paphiopedilum* remain at risk. Once commonly seen for sale in orchid nurseries, *P. fairrieanum*, for example, has virtually disappeared from the wild; and at one time the UK population of *Cypripedium calceolus* was reduced to a single plant in the wild due to over-collection for gardens.

When thinking about conservation, it is easy to become despondent. It is not all bad news, however. *Cypripedium calceolus* was rescued at the last minute by the Sainsbury Orchid Conservation Project at the Royal Botanic Gardens, Kew. Plants were successfully raised from seed and reintroduced into suitably secure sites in the north of England.

Despite the many setbacks, there does appear to be a heartening increase in environmental awareness. People often love and take pride in their native orchid flora, and many countries have an orchid as their national flower. Following Singapore's successful urban orchids reintroduction project, Fairchild Tropical Botanic Garden has instigated the Million Orchid Project in south Florida. The scheme includes a strong educational component, and involves scientists, conservationists and, most importantly, members of the local community including schoolchildren.

It appears that today only two small populations of this striking slipper orchid (*Paphiopedilum fairrieanum*) remain in the wild in Asia.

There are numerous other projects around the globe, with many aimed at preserving rare and threatened habitats. Orchid seed banks such as Kew's Millennium Seed Bank act as insurance policies against future losses and provide material for the reintroduction of species into their native habitats or enhancing remaining populations. They are therefore of utmost importance for orchid conservation.

Troubleshooting

No matter how much care you take, you will find the occasional pest feasting on your plants or, more rarely, a disease attacking them. The key to success in keeping the problem to a minimum is to be vigilant and to act promptly as soon as you do find anything wrong. Prevention is always better than cure.

- As a matter of routine pick up and inspect your plants regularly for signs of pests. Do not forget to look underneath the leaves. Peel back dead sheaths on pseudobulbs of cattleyas and laelias. You may be surprised by what you find.
- Clean leaves regularly (see Cleaning, page 31). Not only will this remove pests, but it will also allow more light to reach the plant tissues – essential for photosynthesis.
- Examine all new acquisitions carefully, and possibly quarantine them for a while until you are confident that they are not secretly harbouring an unwanted visitor.
- Good greenhouse hygiene is essential (see Cleaning, page 31–2) so remove all plant debris regularly.
- Place mesh over greenhouse vents (but not so fine that it interferes with air movement) to impede the entry of large insects such as bees, which may decide to pollinate your flowers.

PESTS

Aphids

These pests seem to appear out of nowhere and at any time of the year, particularly on flowers and fresh new growths. Where they occur on flowers they can cause unsightly brown spotting. Aphids have an alarming ability to multiply rapidly – the females giving birth to live young without the necessity for fertilization. They are sap-suckers, tapping into the phloem (the nutrient-carrying vessels) and may pass on debilitating plant viruses. Plant fluids are rich in sugars but poor in proteins, and aphids excrete a sweet, energy-rich honeydew from their rear ends that both attracts ants and encourages the growth of sooty moulds that can block the pores on the undersides of plant leaves. Ants deliberately farm aphids for

Pest control kit

Make up a simple pest control kit that can be deployed at short notice. This can consist of: a (×10) hand lens or magnifying glass, a soft artist's paintbrush, an old toothbrush, a sharp pointed cane or toothpick, some paper towel and a screw-top jar filled with 50 per cent methylated spirits (rubbing alcohol).

Gone are the days when growers routinely sprayed with noxious chemicals as a preventative measure 'just in case'. Although we all wish to eliminate, or at least keep the use of, harmful chemical insecticides to a minimum, you may want to keep insecticidal soap or an insecticide to hand.

Mealybugs often hide in the crowns of moth orchids (*Phalaenopsis*). Inspect your plants regularly, and treat any signs of infestation promptly.

their honeydew, and will nest in plant pots so be very vigilant.

Aphids are a particular problem in spring. In the home and in the greenhouse, look out for their tell-tale white exoskeletons on leaf surfaces, search out and remove with finger and thumb, or a soft paintbrush dipped in 50 per cent methylated spirits. In the garden, large numbers of aphids are consumed by ladybirds. They are formidable aphid predators, both in their larval and adult stages, so encourage them by providing suitable habitats.

Mealybugs and scale insects

All too commonly found on moth orchids (*Phalaenopsis*), mealybugs resemble miniature armadillos, with a waterproof covering of white waxy filaments. Their eggs are found in white fluffy masses. In the home, dig them out with a toothpick, or treat with a soft paintbrush dipped in 50 per cent methylated spirits. In a greenhouse, control mealybugs by introducing the Australian predatory ladybird *Cryptolaemus montrouzieri*.

Scale insects, which are closely related to mealybugs, cling tightly to plants like miniature limpets. There are a number of species that attack orchids. Boisduval scale (*Diaspis boisduvalii*) can be difficult to eradicate but with patience and persistence can be eliminated by scrubbing affected pseudobulbs regularly with an old toothbrush dipped in 50 per cent methylated spirits, until they no longer reappear. Scale insects can be a particularly serious problem for cattleya lovers, as they hide beneath the papery sheaths surrounding the mature pseudobulbs. Often the first sign of an infestation is the appearance of distinctive, rounded, yellow patches on the leaves, caused by their toxic saliva. Turn the leaf over, and you will find the culprits. The males are easily recognized: they are rectangular, each with three parallel ridges along their length, and they tend to congregate in white fluffy masses. When mature, they undergo a final moult emerging as winged insects that fly off to fertilize the females.

Red spider mites

These mites are commonly found on cymbidiums and thin-leaved orchids. They are indeed members of the spider family, and in extreme infestations the undersides of leaves will be covered by webbing. Usually, the first symptoms will be silvering of the undersides of leaves, which can turn brown as cells become infected with bacteria. Unless you have extremely good eyesight, red spider mites are visible only with the aid of a magnifying glass or a hand lens. They thrive in hot dry conditions, so growing plants in humid conditions will reduce the problem.

To remove them, gently sponge down the leaves, taking care not to pull out the leaves of any new shoots. In a greenhouse, you could try a biological control by introducing the mite predator *Phytoseiulus persimilis.*

Slugs and snails

An orchid grower's worst nightmare is to have their plants attacked by slugs and snails, which can completely consume a tray of precious seedlings in one sitting. Damage to leaves lasts for many years, and blemishes on flowers often prevent growers from exhibiting plants at orchid shows. Rarely an issue indoors, you must be constantly vigilant where plants are being cultivated in a greenhouse or in the garden. These molluscs appear to be able to sniff out flowers and tender new growths, and to be attracted to the aroma given off by damaged foliage. Being able to abseil down the slenderest of threads, they can reach plants suspended in baskets or mounted on bark. Masters of camouflage, snails are also creatures of habit, returning to the same spot each morning. With patience and persistence they can be found. At the first sign of damage, hunt them down mercilessly. Close examination of your plants may reveal your prey in a crevice in a plant mounted on bark, or hiding under the greenhouse staging.

Slugs, unlike snails, will usually return to the scene of the crime

TOP Snails and slugs are arguably the No.1 pest, and can cause a lot of damage. Seek them out with a torch in the evening.

ABOVE Beware of bacterial infections. The infected material should be cut away promptly with a sterile knife and disposed of.

soon after it gets dark. Go into your greenhouse with a torch and look for them in the early evening after the sun has gone down. If you still cannot find them, tip the affected plant out of its pot – slugs frequently hide in the bottoms of pots. They can be kept out by placing a mesh over any drainage holes.

Growers sometimes lure slugs and snails out of hiding with a dish of stale beer or halved potatoes, and dispose of them appropriately once caught. Everyone seems to have their favourite trap. Another control method is to use ferric phosphate pellets as bait, following the manufacturer's instructions. In the garden slugs and snails can be deterred by adding a layer of chopped pine, spruce or larch needles on the soil around precious plants.

Thrips

The first sign of an infestation may be flower damage, with petals and sepals developing small, speckled, pale patches; or else slight scarring of tender new leaves. Close examination may reveal the culprits: tiny, slender, brown or black, winged insects, 1–3mm/1⁄16–1⁄8in long, that feed by stabbing the surface layer of cells and sucking up their contents. They lay their eggs in soft plant tissues. Although the thick waxy cuticle of many orchid leaves may be relatively immune to damage, thrips are especially fond of infecting flower buds, often leading to severe deformation of the flowers.

Monitor for their presence using yellow or blue sticky traps. Tapping plants over a sheet of clean white paper will reveal the presence of any greenish black specks of thrip frass (insect faeces). Although very mobile, thrips can easily be picked off one by one with a brush moistened with water or methylated spirits, and wiped on to a piece of paper towel, for dispatch. Control heavy infestations using insecticidal soaps.

DISEASES

Bacterial rots

Deal with a plant immediately if wet brown spots appear on its leaves, particularly the tips, or if its pseudobulbs become brown and soft. Remove all the affected area with a sharp sterile knife, revealing fresh green tissue. Allow the exposed area to air-dry before resuming watering.

Fungal spotting on flowers

A humid stagnant atmosphere provides ideal conditions for the germination of fungal spores, which can lead to unsightly spotting on flowers. Avoid this by ensuring that you have good air movement in a greenhouse (or basement), by using a fan.

Viruses

Viruses such as cymbidium mosaic virus and odontoglossum ringspot cause a range of symptoms including so-called flower colour break, where the blooms become disfigured. They can be spread from plant to plant by sucking pests such as aphids (see page 134) or be passed on by contaminated tools. Therefore, always use sterile knives or secateurs to cut flower spikes and other parts. To sterilize equipment see Equipment, page 24.

What to do when

SPRING

With progressively longer days and the sun gradually climbing higher in the sky, it is time to think about shading. It can be a tricky time of year, as the weather can be very unpredictable. However, you do not want your plants to suffer from the effects of too much sun.

- Consider repositioning orchids to a shadier windowsill.
- In a greenhouse, apply shading early enough to prevent temperatures from getting too high, and leaves getting scorched, but also to take advantage of increasing light levels. It is a matter of achieving the right balance.
- Spring clean inside and outside a greenhouse. Sweep the floor and remove any debris (see Cleaning, page 31–2).
- Repot when new roots begin to appear and new growths to emerge.
- Do not be over-enthusiastic with the watering. The compost should be moist rather than wet, otherwise pseudobulbs may rot. Do not water dendrobiums until you are sure any flower buds have passed the point of no return and will not turn into keikis (see page 36).
- Check plants regularly as temperatures increase and pests become increasingly active and multiply rapidly. Look out for aphids (see page 134) on flower buds, and slugs and snails (see page 136) sneaking into a greenhouse from the garden.
- Clean leaves (see Cleaning, page 31–2).
- Peel back and remove dead sheaths of cattleyas and their relatives, checking for scale insects (see Mealybugs and scale insects, page 135), which may have insinuated themselves underneath .
- Purchase plants for your home, greenhouse or garden.
- Plant out hardy varieties, but beware of late frosts. Give plants additional protection – a cloche, for example.
- Collect and store rainwater whenever the opportunity arises. As it is a precious resource, use it judiciously.

SUMMER

The sun is now at its highest and strongest, and the further from the equator you travel the longer the days are.

- Store tubers of bee orchid (*Ophrys apifera*) and blunt greenhood (*Pterostylis curta*), once the foliage has died down, somewhere cool and dark (see Bee orchid, page 100, and Blunt greenhood, page 113).
- Move orchids away from a sunny window to an east- or west-facing one, or increase the shade, as appropriate for each plant.
- Water copiously as most plants will be growing at their maximum rate. For sympodial plants with pseudobulbs, the aim is to build plump pseudobulbs before their winter rest. Monopodials will add more foliage and perhaps branching fans of leaves.

Pests, especially scale insects, can sometimes be found beneath the dry sheaths of the pseudobulbs of *Laelia anceps* and orchids in related genera. Removal of the dry sheaths is recommended.

- Feed epiphytes in the greenhouse or on the windowsill with a balanced fertilizer at half-strength, to rapidly produce bright green growth. Towards the end of summer, change to a high-potash fertilizer (tomato feed) to encourage stronger, disease-resistant growth and to promote flowering (see individual plant profiles, pages 38–129).
- Ensure automatic vents are opening on warm sunny days in a greenhouse. You may also need to open under-bench ventilators and, if the weather is very hot, the greenhouse door, too.
- Damp down the greenhouse floor regularly with watering cans of tap water, to mitigate the loss of humidity because of vents being open.
- Spray plants early in the morning so the foliage can dry before the sun is at its strongest.
- Move (usually cooler-growing) orchids from the greenhouse or home to a shady spot (for relevant species see individual plant profiles, pages 38–129).
- Ensure the soil remains moist in the garden by watering especially in dry spells. Do this early in the morning or in early evening.

AUTUMN

Days are getting shorter. This is a time when many orchids are approaching their winter rest. Pseudobulbs have almost completed their growth. The leaves of deciduous orchids begin to turn yellow, before being shed.

Regular damping down of the greenhouse floor helps to maintain a high relative humidity. This is especially important in hot weather.

- Reduce watering and fertilizing gradually.
- Decrease the degree of greenhouse shading gradually until it is no longer needed.
- Clean the glass inside and out in a greenhouse or cold frame.
- Replace (bubble-wrap) insulation where necessary to make the most of the reduced light.
- Seal any draughts in a greenhouse – plants do not appreciate a cold draught and neither do you want to lose heat from a greenhouse in winter.
- Continue to damp down the greenhouse floor.
- Bring any plants that have been summering outdoors into a greenhouse or indoors, before the first frosts.
- Once their canes (pseudobulbs) have completed their growth, place *nobile*-type dendrobiums (see Noble orchid, page 77) somewhere cool and dry over winter to stimulate flowering in the following spring.
- Check tubers weekly of wintergreen terrestrials that have been stored over the summer somewhere cool and dark. Pot them up when they begin to sprout.
- Clear away foliage as it begins to die down in the garden.
- Protect vulnerable plants with cloches.
- Plant many tuberous orchids (if appropriate) and cypripediums, giving them time to become established before winter sets in.

WINTER

Winter is a magical but potentially challenging season. Magical because, although there is little in flower outdoors in the garden, many plants are coming into flower indoors. It is challenging because the short days, in temperate regions at least, are often accompanied by many days with grey skies, meaning that the amount of available light is poor.

- Windowsill growers need to be aware of the dangers of cold nights, and move plants away from cold windowsills, especially overnight.
- Grow plants on humidity trays or set up some companion planting (see Companion planting on a windowsill, page 58) to counterbalance the dry atmosphere in a centrally heated home, which can lead to bud drop.
- Look for new inflorescences in a greenhouse. There is little more annoying than to find a slug has found them first.

ABOVE Standing your orchids on a tray containing moist gravel helps to maintain a humid atmosphere around your plants.
RIGHT Stanhopeas flower from the base of the plant, and should be grown in baskets.

- Water plants only when appropriate. This can be challenging because you have to decide in many cases whether to do so. It is the time of year when many plants need a distinct winter rest. Cool-growers, on the other hand, are liable to be very happy, and will continue growing until their pseudobulbs are fully made up.
- Maintain a humid atmosphere in a heated greenhouse. If you are fortunate enough to heat your greenhouse with old-fashioned, cast-iron hot-water pipes, then you will be able to maintain that wonderful damp greenhouse aroma without too many problems. Electric fan heaters, on the other hand, dry out the atmosphere, particularly when the weather outdoors is very cold, and the heaters are running a lot of the time. Remedy the lack of humidity by regular damping down, and having trays filled with water set on a greenhouse floor. Use water that is the same temperature as the greenhouse.
- In the garden most of your orchids will be dormant. Ventilate plants in a cold frame when the weather allows.
- Ensure orchid compost remains slightly moist, but not wet. With a few exceptions, composts should not be allowed to dry out to the stage where it is difficult or impossible to re-wet.

Index

Page numbers in *italics* indicate text in a box or an illustration. Page numbers in **bold** indicate a main entry for that plant.

Quarto

First published in 2020 by Frances Lincoln,
an imprint of The Quarto Group.
One Triptych Place,
London, SE1 9SH,
United Kingdom
T (0)20 7700 9000
www.Quarto.com

This edition published in 2026 by Frances Lincoln.

EEA Representation, WTS Tax d.o.o., Žanova ulica 3, 4000
Kranj, Slovenia
www.wts-tax.si

A catalogue record for this book is available from the British Library.

ISBN 978-1-80570-034-0
Ebook ISBN 978-0-71124-281-4

10 9 8 7 6 5 4 3 2 1

Design by Arianna Osti

Printed in Guangdong, China TT102025

MIX
Paper | Supporting responsible forestry
FSC® C016973
FSC www.fsc.org

Acknowledgments

Although the author tends to get all the credit, the truth is that any book is a collaborative venture, involving many people behind the scenes without whom it would not be completed, and still less published.

One of the most enjoyable aspects of writing this book has been the interest and encouragement given to me by friends in the orchid world. I want to thank Joyce, my lovely wife especially, for her continued support and patience with her husband's orchid obsession, and for writing the project about how to make an orchid corsage. I would also like to thank Pei Chu for her diligence in searching out suitable images, Arianna Osti for her design work producing such an attractive layout, and Michael Brunström, the in-house project editor; Joanna Chisholm for keeping me on the straight and narrow, when I tended to wander off-message; and Gina Fullerlove and Helen Griffin for persuading me to write the book in the first place.

Photographic acknowledgements

a=above; b=below; m=middle; l=left; r=right

© **Alamy** 42 REDA &CO srl, 70 Minden, 103al PhotoAlto sas, 122 Alan Gregg, 141l Avalon/Photoshot License

© **Chris Barker** 14/2

© **GAP Photos** 103ml John Swithinbank, 103br, 103bl Friedrich Strauss

© **Getty Images** 103ar Fabrice Lerouge

© **Jason Ingram** 2, 6–7, 10r, 26, 33, 38–9, 45tl+tr+ml, 51, 59ar, 66, 73, 85, 91, 95, 109, 117, 125

© **Michael Bull** 14/3, 106, 107

© **Philip Seaton** 10l, 11, 13l, 13r, 14/1, 14/4, 19, 21, 22, 29, 34, 37, 45mr+b, 55ar+bl, 62, 69, 80, 97, 105, 114, 123, 126, 132b, 139, 140, 141r

© **Ray Tunnicliff** 48

© **Shutterstock** 17 ForGaby, 25 neung_pongsak, 30 lieber, 32 New Africa, 40 Hanjo Hellmann, 41 guentermanaus, 47 RowanArtCreation, 52 Zach Martin, 55br Salparadis, 59al Tatjana Michaljova, 59b Sharaf Maksumov, 71 Jiri Prochanzka, 81 DM Larson, 82 eera5607, 83 guentermanaus, 89 Martina Simonazzi, 90 Martin Fowler, 93 Ricardo de Paula Ferreria, 100 Bildagentur Zoonar GmbH, 111 GiDes Photography, 113 Martin Fowler, 115 chutima chaimratana, 119 Nick Pecker, 127 Sergey Lapin, 128 guentermanaus, 130 Elnur, 133 Martin Fowler, 135 FCerez, 136a niphon thammincha, 136b Chayangkul Issadej